VIRAL

MYTHOLOGY

HOW THE TRUTH OF THE ANCIENTS
WAS ENCODED AND PASSED DOWN THROUGH
LEGEND, ART, AND ARCHITECTURE

MARIE D. JONES *and* LARRY FLAXMAN

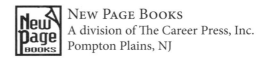

NEW PAGE BOOKS
A division of The Career Press, Inc.
Pompton Plains, NJ

VIRAL MYTHOLOGY
EDITED BY JODI BRANDON
TYPESET BY EILEEN MUNSON
Cover design by Zoe Shtorm
Printed in the U.S.A.

To order this title, please call toll-free 1-800-CAREER-1 (NJ and Canada: 201-848-0310) to order using VISA or MasterCard, or for further information on books from Career Press.

The Career Press, Inc.
220 West Parkway, Unit 12
Pompton Plains, NJ 07444
www.careerpress.com
www.newpagebooks.com

Library of Congress Cataloging-in-Publication Data

CIP Data Available Upon Request.

❧

*This book is dedicated to
Max Jones and Mary Essa Flaxman.
The information of the past and present
is theirs to build a better future with.
May they use it well.*

❧

Acknowledgments

Marie and Larry would like to acknowledge Lisa Hagan, our amazing agent, who is a superhero who makes things happen! Thank you, Lisa, for everything! To Michael and Laurie Pye and the team at New Page Books, you guys ROCK. Thanks for another chance to spread our gospel and have fun doing it! To the amazing team at Warwick Associates, you make us look so good! To all the people who contributed to this book, we appreciate your time and insights more than we can say. And to our fans and followers and friends and radio hosts and supporters, and even our enemies, you guys make it all worthwhile; we thank you from the bottom of our hearts!

Marie wishes to also thank:

To my mom, Milly, who never ceases to be there for me and is always supportive and loving, the best things a mom could ever be. What would I do without you? And to my dad, John, who watches from heaven, smiling, thanks for all you instilled in me and taught me. To my sister and best friend, Angella, you are my support column and confidante and so much more! To my brother, John, thanks for all your humor and craziness! To my dear friends, my writer colleagues, and my Wahines, what would I do without any of you?

Let me once again thank Larry Flaxman, for the long conversations that lead to new ideas, for the laughs, the friendship, the sad times we picked each other up, the happy times we bubbled over with excitement, for the long and frustrating periods of hard work, and then waiting for the payoffs, for pushing me to think deeper and wider and bigger and challenging me to do better and be a better person, and for all the amazing good times that await us as we venture forth into new territory. I treasure it all, Larry. Are you sick of me yet? There is so much more to come!

And to my son, Max, who is my universe, my sun, my moon, my heart, and my soul. Everything I do, I do it for you.

Larry would like to thank:

There are so many amazing people in my life that attempting to cram them all into a few paragraphs is impossible. With that being said, please know that I am eternally grateful, and would like to apologize in advance if I have failed to mention your name.

Firstly, I would like to thank my mom, Sheila, and my dad, Norman, for providing such a loving, nurturing childhood and upbringing. Those formative years have absolutely instilled in me the qualities and traits that have served to mold and form me into the man I am today. I am so incredibly honored to be your son and learn from the best. Not a day goes by that I don't miss seeing or hearing your voices. I love you both more than words, and look forward to the day that we will be reunited in "The Grid."

I would also like to thank my wife, Emily, for understanding (and tolerating!) my often-hectic working hours and crazy travel schedule. I can't even imagine how difficult it must be!

In addition, I am extremely thankful to all of my friends, fans, and associates that provide me with advice, comments, ideas, and motivation. You folks make the long hours and sleepless nights worthwhile!

Marie D. Jones, I don't even know where to start. I look back over the last six years and continue to be amazed at what we have been able to accomplish together. We absolutely make one hell of a team! Despite both experiencing profound loss last year, we have managed to rise above, and motivate, inspire, and encourage not only others, but each other. I am so incredibly thankful that you are in my life. You are truly a wonderful friend, and I am so honored to not only call you my friend, but to work exclusively with you. My mom always used to say, "To health, wealth, and happiness!" and I couldn't agree more.

So this brings us to the last and most significant person that I would like to thank: my daughter, Mary Essa. I am so proud to call you my daughter. Words cannot even describe how much you mean to me. Every time I look in your eyes I see a window to my own soul. Your sense of wonderment mirrors and parallels my own, and I look forward to many more exciting adventures with you. I love you more than life itself!

Contents

Collective Consciousness and Cloud Computing
by Heather Lynn, PhD

Consider for a moment a smartphone, laptop, and a desktop computer. Though individually different in appearance and function, these devices can often communicate with one another. In recent years, there has been a move toward cloud computing, whereby varying electronic devices can share and retrieve data through a remote source. In my point of view, this is somewhat analogous to the way information seemed to "go viral" among humans during ancient times. I call it the "Cosmic Cloud Computing" theory. However, by only looking at the material evidence that is found in the archaeological record, we may actually limit our understanding of how information spread in the ancient world.

First, we must establish how truly limited our knowledge of history is. Though primary schools may imply otherwise, our narrative of ancient cultures has only recently been written. Apart from a handful of religious texts, comparably few primary sources exist in the historical record about the lives and cultures of some of the earliest civilizations. Our current understanding of these civilizations is due in large part to the careful reconstruction of evidence from excavations and the subsequent analysis of artifacts. The greatest majority of this research has only been in the past few hundred years—just a speck on the time line of the history of man.

Originally seen as a hobby, *antiquarianism*, as it was initially called, has been around since at least the first millennium BCE, as noted in ancient Greek texts that ponder lost technologies based on stone. Inquiry into the past has likely always been a part of human interests. People have searched for missing treasures and artifacts since prehistory and have routinely looted graves. However, the transformation of this informal activity into a science did not take place until the 17th and 18th centuries CE.

The first systematic archaeological excavations are considered to have taken place in the 18th century, beginning with three significant sites: the Roman cities of Herculaneum and Pompeii in 1738, Thomas Jefferson's excavations in Virginia in 1784, and Napoleon's famous Egyptian excavations in 1798. The study of these sites eventually led to a boon of discoveries in the years ahead, from the Sumerian discoveries in 1899 to the discoveries of the Minoan, Olmec, and so on.

Organizational efforts started to occur with the formation of antiquarian societies in the 19th century. Many of these societies observed basic guidelines regarding the classification of artifacts, the use of field notes and photography to record excavations, and the publication of results. It is also in these societies that we see the beginning of cooperative excavation and concern for the rights of indigenous people.

Upon reflection, it becomes shockingly apparent just how new archaeology is. The science of archaeology and related discoveries hit critical mass in the early part of the 20th century and has snowballed ever since. This has led to some of the most important and magnificent archaeological discoveries ever made. Still, archaeology continues to develop both as a science and as a profession, as does our understanding of our collective past. So how does archaeology explain the transmission of common themes in myths, legends, art, structures, and belief systems of the ancient world? Not adequately and certainly not conclusively. As our knowledge of the past is continuously changing, so are our theories and explanations.

The best place to begin examining the transmission of communication in ancient history is in Mesopotamia. This encompasses the area between the Tigris and Euphrates rivers in what is now Iraq. By at least the fourth millennium BCE, the first urban cultures started to form. These early civilizations included the Sumerians, Akkadians, Babylonians, and Assyrians. A substantial amount of knowledge has been gained from these civilizations due to their meticulous record-keeping.

In Mesopotamia, as well as in Egypt, there was a quickening of cultural development and a population increase in the last centuries of the fourth millennium BCE. In a blink of an eye (about 300 years), we see complex structures, theologies, and written languages emerge. The reasons for this quickening remain a mystery and are still being debated by scholars. However, one school of thought is that advances in these civilizations were brought about by incursions of people from Western Asia. Some researchers believe in the existence of an "Asiatic Invasion" that transformed an earlier African culture and established the foundations on which the dynastic state was brought about. However, this view has no firm support in the archaeological record. This is not to imply that there was no contact. There is little doubt about the cultural relations between Egypt and Western Asia. Many researchers believe that relationships in these regions were greatly intensified over this short amount of time due to increased contact brought about by the development of sturdier seagoing ships.

Another explanation for the rise of civilization in both Mesopotamia and Egypt is the irrigation hypothesis. This theory suggests that competition for water resources increased the need for laborers and spurred the development of a bureaucracy to manage the growing labor force.

This ultimately led to the rise of a state superstructure evident in the building of temples and administrative centers. Increasing centralization of economic activity demanded the development of a complex recording system, as we find in the Sumerian cylinder seals and the thousands of cuneiform tablets that record business transactions of local and long-distance trade.

In turn, the need for job specialization such as professional scribes, craftsmen, managers, priests, and others at high levels of government illustrates the necessary shift from the use of tribal laws toward more centralized state governance. This shift is often referred to as the "Urban Revolution" and could be responsible for creating a more unified culture in the region.

These seem like logical theories to explain how information could travel among a diverse cross-section of people. That is, until you consider that at approximately the same time on the other side of the globe, other cultures experienced similar rapid advancements in technology, art, and society. Take the Olmec, for example. According to the archeological record, the Olmec civilization just suddenly appeared from around 1200 BCE. There seems to have been no gradual sequence of local growth in the region. Clearly there has been no simple explanation for Olmec origins or their evolution. What we do know is that it expanded rapidly between 1200 BCE and 800 BCE, and that the Olmec symbols and artifacts are present in several distinct areas such as Honduras and Costa Rica. Did artistic and creative elements of Olmec civilization develop somewhere else and get transported to Mexico?

Some researchers believe this may be the case, and have even pointed out some similarities in art and myths between Mesoamerican and Mesopotamian culture. A minority of them have theorized that the spread of information in these regions was so rapid that an invisible hand of an invading civilization must have been responsible. However, this could be viewed as too speculative or presumptuous because, for as many similarities as we may find, there are just as many, if not more, differences. For example, many ancient writing systems were similarly pictographic, but upon in-depth study, clear differences can be identified.

So what does archaeology teach us about the spread of information in the ancient world? Not as much as mainstream archaeologists and historians would have us believe. Ultimately, the majority of history is still a mystery. According to Thomas Edison, "We don't know one-millionth of one percent about anything." I would venture to say that this is a fair assessment. We can only gain a more holistic understanding of human history by using an interdisciplinary approach to study, like what is being done by Marie D. Jones and Larry Flaxman in this book. My passion for cooperative research is why my personal theory on the viral transmission of communication in ancient history leans more in the direction of the spiritual or philosophical, rather than purely archaeological.

This leads me to my personal theory of "Cosmic Cloud Computing." Admittedly not entirely supported by the archaeological record, it is partially supported across a number of other fields such as metaphysics, psychology, biology, and quantum theory. Rene Descartes believed there was only one conscious mind. Carl Jung expanded on this thought by introducing the concept of the collective unconscious. Modern scientists, such as Rupert Sheldrake, have suggested that nature, in general, has memory that can be described as telepathic. All of these theories point to the idea that there is interconnectedness among all living things and possible collective memories within each species.

Aristotle said, "Nature operates in the shortest way possible." Rather than trying to reconstruct the past by filling in the blanks, let's use Occam's razor to dissect the complex creations of past civilizations and try to recognize basic underlying concepts. Take the example of the "Golden Rule." Most are familiar with this basic ethical tenet. It tells us to treat people how we would like to be treated. Following is a table that illustrates some of the numerous recorded versions of this tenet, spanning cultures, time, and geography.

The Universality of the Golden Rule

Confucianism	"What you don't want done to yourself, don't do to others." —*Analects 15:23*
Buddhism	"Hurt not others with that pains thyself." —*Udana-Varga 5: 18*
Hinduism	"Do naught to other which if done to thee would cause thee pain." —*Mahabharata 5:1517*
Zoroastrianism	"Do not do unto others all that which is not well for oneself." —*Shayast-na-Shayast 13:29*
Ancient Egyptian	"That which you hate to be done to you, do not do to another." —*The Tale of the Eloquent Peasant, 109–110, translated from a Late Period (c. 664 BC –323 BC) Egyptian papyrus*
Classical Paganism	"May I do to other as I would that they do unto me." —*Plato*
Judaism	"What is hateful to you; do not to your fellow man. This is the law: all the rest is commentary." —*Talmud, Shabbat 31a*
Christianity	"Therefore all things whatsoever ye would that men should do to you, do ye even so to them: for this is the law and the prophets." —*Matthew 7:12 (King James Version)*
Islam	"None of you [truly] believes until he wishes for his brother what he wishes for himself." —*Number 13 of Imam Al-Nawawi's Forty Hadiths*
Native America Spirituality	"Do not wrong or hate your neighbor. For it is not he who you wrong, but yourself." —*Pima proverb*

All of these examples are written in different styles with varying complexities and originating in unique languages. Apart from all of these differences, there is a unified message of empathic reciprocity. Considering what the archaeological record shows about possible diffusion, migration, trade, and expansion, it still does not fully explain the consistency in the underlying message. When stripped of cultural identity, the message remains the same. Are we to believe that the "Golden Rule" is instinctual? Is it an innate principal? If so, where does it originate?

Jung believed that we experience the unconscious through symbols. This includes the products of all art, music, and language, both written and oral. Given the astounding consistency in the underlying themes of these symbols, perhaps there is a collective memory being transmitted, evocative of the Memes in Greek mythology, universally expressed through the creations of humans.

Archetypal symbols are mysteriously transmitted throughout history and modernity. Nevertheless, it is not a question of specific inherited images as much as it is one of a unified conscious experience. The interaction between our individual perceptions, universal consciousness, and symbolism enriches life and promotes personal development and growth.

Going back to my analogy of cloud computing, imagine that there is a universal consciousness filled with infinite data. All organisms, unique in design and function, are wired in such a way that they can tap into this "Cosmic Cloud" to send and retrieve data. Likewise, we can communicate with each other, but to do so requires an interface or the use of symbols. Which symbols we use depends on a number of factors unique to our individual abilities and limitations. However, as in the example of the "Golden Rule," a unified message of mysterious origin can still be found underneath the symbols. Core messages seem consistent and enduring, even after the death of an individual or entire civilization. The information does not die along with the computing device or organism. Just as if your laptop were to no longer function, you can be sure that there are still people accessing their e-mail and streaming media online somewhere else in the world.

People do travel, communicate, and spread ideas and symbols. This is an indisputable fact. It can be proven in the archaeological record as well as in numerous other fields of study. Likewise, our smartphone can sync with tablets and our tablets can sync with desktop computers, and so on. The transmission of this data can appear to be purely physical. If someone were to observe the sharing of data between two smartphones and not know or understand the unseen details behind that process, it would appear that the two devices simply independently communicated with each other because they were of similar design and function, and in close proximity. This is essentially what we do when we focus solely on the physical or material evidence left behind by ancient cultures. We interpret out of the artifacts, rather than looking in.

These perspectives are not mutually exclusive. Like modern computing devices, we can and do physically share information when we are in close proximity. However, it is my belief that there are also unseen, immaterial factors, as suggested in the research and theories of Rene Descartes, Carl Jung, and Rupert Sheldrake. The question of how ancient people seemed to rapidly transmit themes in art, myth, and religion, regardless of geographic or technological restrictions, can only be answered if we view the universe as greater than ourselves.

Heather Lynn, PhD, is a writer, researcher, speaker, and archeologist with a PhD in comparative religion. She is president and founder of the Society for Truth in Archeological Research and a member of the World Archeological Congress. Her latest book is Anthrotheology: Searching For God in Man, *and she researches and speaks widely on hidden history, mythology, esotericism, and the origin of consciousness. Her Website is* www.drheatherlynn.com.

A Perception of Ancient Symbolism
From an Adventurous Egyptologist
by John R. Ward

During the past few years I have been privileged to be part of research, which has identified a growing need to further understand the significance of ancient symbolism as it continues to accompany us in these modern times. This symbolism plays at the core of what makes us human beings, and comprises an integral part in the creation, development, and sustainment of our collective psyche.

As human beings we have surrounded ourselves with belief systems, and their accompanying guidelines-to-living. We have done this to offer guidance, to answer questions we perceive as unanswerable, and to bring us peace of mind when we can no longer rationalize the situations our world presents us. The human race has seen itself become organized into a diverse and complex social caste structure, disciplined into an attempt to bring order to our environment in which we have no control over. Due to this contradictory nature of the structure of our existence, we find ourselves curious to push the boundaries of our conscious awareness of our surroundings.

During this interplay we, as human beings, have developed a structured system of ICONS and IMAGES to which we can all relate as a human race, no matter where we are or what we call ourselves. This imagery encodes the fundamentals within either the society to which we are directly connected, or to a more UNIVERSAL CULTURAL SETTING.

The symbols we find ourselves surrounded by are used as a tool of interaction with one another on a non-verbal level, which requires no personal conscious thought process. Our conditioned mindsets interpret the symbolism on an individual basis through a series of stages of emotional, psychological responses. The symbolism corresponds to pictorial units, which do not necessarily have any natural resemblance. A single image may range from symbolizing a minor cultural aspect to a fully developed, global ideology. The symbols trigger an IMMEDIATE AND OUTSTANDING SUBLIMINAL REACTION when we are confronted by receiving their communicated message.

The very use of symbolism to communicate a message to one another has been inherent in our social structure and has evolved with us. However, throughout time, the FUNDAMENTAL IMAGERY HAS NOT DIFFERED THAT MUCH. *(The use of geometric configurations and straight recognizable lines of reference have been passed on to us through several generations.)* Even without realizing it, we still recognize and affiliate ourselves with cave etchings and drawings thousands of years old. Their influence over us continued even as their origins and early appearances disappeared. However, the subliminal interaction and acceptance lies within us constantly, dormant but ever-present.

Modern-day Egypt holds an abundance of the world's ancient archaeological remains, which has shaped in one way or another the Western world's perception of esoteric and hermetic teachings; yet approximately 90 percent of ancient Egypt still remains hidden beneath the sands of time. Imagine the wealth of knowledge and wisdom that remains undiscovered and what this cache of ancient understanding could bring to our own belief systems. What we can see today, though, is a veritable feast upon the eyes, stimulating our senses and emotions, and in some cases transcending us on a journey through history, as if we were somehow an integral part of something much larger.

The hieroglyphs, architectural elements, and stunning divine iconography all blend into one cacophony of symbolism, an orchestrated movement, which stirs the inner soul. We are aroused by this experience and taken to various levels of pleasure that for some feels alien and awkward, but intriguing and sensual at the same time.

There are many questions that arise from such a mystical appraisal; were the ancient Egyptians aware of the intent that they had placed within their art and architectural forms? Was it their aim to place within these elements a message that could be conveyed and read by those who were not necessarily initiated into the Hermetic wisdom texts of the God Thoth?

Egyptian symbolism has long captivated the minds of philosophers and academicians alike, attempting in vain to re-capture the esoteric essence that lies within the ruins of Egypt. Secret societies, cults, religions, and industrial families had all adopted the ancient Egyptian craft as if it holds at its core the very material building blocks of life itself. Pyramids, sphinxes, lotus-budded columns and architraves, ankhs and serpentine crowns have all adorned our upper echelons of society, emulating the grandeur and spectacle of a great and magnificent lost civilization, but again in a vain attempt to invoke a certain transition of emotional and extra sensory perception as if a game of power play is at hand. Many a conspiracy theorist would agree!

Having explored the four corners of Egypt and retraced the footsteps of those that once dared to carve a route out of the inhospitable deserts, I have been privileged to observe firsthand the migration and development of ancient symbolic representations. As the caravan routes expanded so did the wisdom and knowledge contained within the pre-existing temple cities that lined the banks of the Grand River Nile.

Established state symbolism, combined with new and superstitious attributes of the fresh surroundings, began to emerge. The merger of old and new symbols held a certain charge that was readily identifiable by those who gazed upon them, understanding and deciphering the code within. It was travelers, tradesmen, armed garrisons, and migrant workers who carried this recently modified alchemistical symbolism with them, integrating them within their own stories of bravery and survival; articulating and passing on further to others their knowledge as the trade routes expanded over to mainland Europe. Europeans then assimilated and integrated this wealth of knowledge and myth within their own tales and belief systems.

So how could symbolism have affected the common man? Was it merely the size of the monumental structures looming in the distance, the home of the Pharaoh, fear of death, punishment, reward, and sacrifice? Was it the fear of the unknown, one of the greatest power plays by man upon man, to instill within him a fear or dread of the darkness that inhabits a soulless body, the Afterlife? Or was it unapproachable artistic symbolism, controlled by the state that kept the common Egyptian from understanding his role in the universe? Are we so different today?

Lest we forget, today we surround ourselves with similar symbolism; in fact, our entire lives are dedicated to symbolism in one way or another. There is little difference between the ancient Egyptians and us. They too were surrounded by symbolism; each and every component of day-to-day living was represented by a symbol or a collection of: Gods, deities, divine apparatus, attributes, spells, magic, religion (state or public), shrines, temples, statues, decrees, stelae, monumental scarabs erected in town squares declaring the voice of the living God, and the Pharaoh. Maybe it is just the interpretation of said symbols that separates us.

Interpretation is the key: While we give something one meaning, someone else will most definitely read it as something else. Personal upbringing, conditioning or cultural and religious effects all make us individuals and play integral parts in our process of interpretation. It goes without saying that the ancient Egyptian life was one of toil and hard work, surviving in a land that was harsh, cruel, and unforgiving. Life expectancies were far lower. For them their time on earth was a preparation for death, the next true life. Death was eternal, and the preparation was paramount to survive and navigate the Underworld. Symbolism, therefore, played an important role, if not pivotal, in the overall undertaking. We have lost the concept of appreciation; we take life for granted, require everything in the here and now and to be served upon a plate to us, and yet we require the rewards for service and obedience in the next world. How can we therefore even begin to compare our modern symbolic world to that of the ancient Egyptian with all of his relevant symbolism? Theirs was truly Ma'at—harmony, truth, and justice—while we dwell in the chaos.

Dr John R. Ward is an archaeologist, anthropologist, explorer, author, public speaker, and radio host from Hereford, England. His new book is The Exodus Reality: Unearthing the Real History of Moses, Identifying the Pharaohs, and Examining the Exodus From Egypt *with Scott A. Roberts. Currently, John is a member of the Gebel el Silsila Survey Project team working at the largest ancient sand stone quarries in Egypt, the source for many of the ancient upper Egyptian temples and shrines. John lives on the West bank of Luxor, the former location of ancient Thebes, famous today for its ancient historical sites and tombs, with his partner and their menagerie of animals.*

Going Viral

It's impossible to go online to any social networking site without running across something that has not gone "viral." Not in the sense of disease, like the Ebola virus or avian flu, but instead a transmission of information in the form of words or images that spreads like a virus all across the world via the Web. And like the most virulent and contagious of viruses, this information makes its way into the minds and hearts of people from all walks of life, should they but click on a particular link or watch a particular video. Then, they pass that information on to their friends and family, who pass it along to theirs, and so on and so on and so on.

Within hours, 15 million people can be made privy to a video of a man lustily eating French fries, or a cat that plays piano, or a talented toddler singing the National Anthem in Aramaic while juggling, blindfolded.

Information today is passed from person to person at a speed that boggles the mind, and would have been thought of as magic during ancient times. Yet even then, somehow information managed to get around, from civilization to civilization, sometimes crossing oceans and vast bodies of land, even uninhabited land, despite the lack of technology to help that spread. No planes, trains, and automobiles...no Pony Express...no mail service...no phones...and certainly no computers and Internet access.

Ancient civilizations had no discernable means of passing their knowledge and history on in a viral sense. Or did they?

Imagine having no computer or phone. Imagine having some information you wanted to get from your neck of the woods to a town a thousand miles away. How would you do that? And what if there was no guarantee anyone would even see it in your lifetime? How could that information be embedded so that someday, someone would see it?

The key would be to embed and transmit that information using the means you had available at the time, of course. Writing, stories, myth, art, architecture, symbolism, even music. Any form of communication would do, as long as there was the promise of it reaching beyond the confines of your own small place in the world. The tools of the past, as crude as they may appear to those of us addicted to our gadgets, included methods and means of embedding knowledge, even scientific and historical information, within fairy tales and cosmogenesis stories, religious parables and stories, myths and folklore, art and buildings, sacred edifices and esoteric objects. Think about the Greek and Roman myths we learned in school. What we have come to know as story often contains more fact than we ever imagined. But that fact is often hidden behind a beginning, a middle, and an end, with a message or a theme, and images describing events that there was no sophisticated verbiage for at the time. Myths and stories are meant to impart information even as it continues a legacy of a people from generation to generation.

This book examines the way stories, myths, and folklore show how even the most primitive cultures understood the world around them far more than we give them credit for. Joseph Campbell's *The Masks of God* proposes that ancient literature, including mythology, actually contained significant scientific concepts and understanding, and are examples of "monomyth," the common structures found in all myth and ancient stories. This literature of ancient times was meant to tell us something. It was information in the form of oral and written tradition.

It was meant to go viral, only much slower because the spread was from mouth to ear, or page to eye.

In addition, *Viral Mythology* looks at "archeoenigmas," intriguing common themes and elements in ancient myth, stories, and even art, architecture, iconography, and symbolism. Stories were often told in pictures, and the images used all over the world to describe various natural phenomena, and even potentially supernatural phenomena, were often similar to one another, suggesting that certain themes were archetypal. Why did so many diverse civilizations, separated by thousands of miles, with no real means or methods of communication, all tell the same stories, and use the same symbolic imagery, with only slight regionally influenced variations? Was there some outside influence spreading these common themes, or were these cultures tapping into a field of ideas and information that existed in the collective subconscious?

Do fairytales and folkloric stories contain real, hard science, or descriptions of real historical events hidden within the tall-tale telling, as understood and interpreted by the authors who wrote them and the cultures that spread them? Often, the story format served to describe the process of birth, life, and death, especially of the natural world, as documented in anthropologist Sir James Frazier's *The Golden Bough,* a massive tome filled with stories of fertility rites, magic, human sacrifice, and nature worship. Frazier's amazing book combined both scientific thought with religious perspectives to present an examination of rituals and symbolism throughout the 20th century, progressing from beliefs in magic to religion to science.

This book also discusses the history of tarot cards and other occult and esoteric tools and symbols that hid ancient and secret knowledge from the powers that be of the day within their mysterious imagery, as well as the use of such symbolism by secret societies and religious orders that often operated under the authoritarian radar. Even some of the great art of the past contains hidden scientific and historic information, waiting to be deciphered and discovered by those with discerning eyes.

We also look at ancient archeological and astronomical edifices, monuments, drawings, and images that attempt to express scientific knowledge through iconography and sacred geometry. As above, so below. From Stonehenge to Chartres Cathedral, from the similarities of pyramid structures all over the world, to images of aliens and entities that are prevalent in even the most diverse of cultures, there is hidden truth to be found in the words and pictures and architecture of the distant past.

Viral Mythology is about the way we communicate the truth, and sometimes even the way that we spread rumors and theories that become the stuff of conspiracy and myth and legend, often by hiding it in the creativity, art, architecture, and the imagination of the times, out of direct sight of those who might not want that truth revealed. This book is also about how the stories we tell create and shape the future, based upon our understanding of the past and present. The tales we tell today become the reality of the next generations. The information that shapes our lives today is the new mythology, one day to be unearthed and rediscovered by a civilization far in the future that will wonder how we, too, went viral with the crude technology of our time. The scientific knowledge and historical events of today will one day serve as the study lessons to those in the future who thirst for an understanding of their own past. They, like us, will look back and wonder if what we are describing in the information we convey is the truth, the whole truth, and nothing but the truth, or a fictionalized version that contains within it our level of understanding of the world around us.

Like us, they will wonder how information was embedded in our stories, movies, TV shows, novels, books, and so on; and they, like us, will attempt to construct an image of what life was like for us primitive folks in their distant past.

We are their past, and the way we communicate information is their study guide, a guide that is no doubt filled with words and images and objects that speak and sing of "the way we were."

In the beginning... Once upon a time... Long ago and far away....

Chapter 1

Information, Please:
How We Spread It, How We Get It

Question: What did they use as means of
transmitting information in the ancient days?
Answer: Men on feet.

—Answers.com

The success of any kind of social epidemic is
heavily dependent on the involvement of people
with a particular and rare set of gifts.
—Malcolm Gladwell

This is a book about information: what it is, how it is spread, and why. Without information, we wouldn't know anything, or be able to express what we know. Without information, we are left in the dark, stumbling for understanding and a footing to stand on. Information is the "stuff" of our reality, from the ideas that fill our heads to the statistics we see on the news to the facts we learn in school to the theories that scientists posit to describe the world we live in and how it works.

All these "its and bits" of information fill our brains with things to perceive and process, and to make sense of the reality we call home, and to imagine the possibilities of other realities as well. Information is education, creativity, intuition, knowledge, wisdom, and fact and all that emerges from the realms of the mind into the physical. Information is everything. The word *information* comes from the Latin *informare*, which means "to inform" or "to give form to the mind." It also means to teach or instruct, and when information is passed on, it is often for the means of instructing or teaching something to the receiver.

But information can also be described as any sensory input to an organism, like a human being. This input is designed to help the organism identify and process the system in which it exists by identifying and using data such as environmental factors and influences, threats to safety, food and water location, changes in social systems, and even the possibility of mating. Some information is meaningless to one organism, but crucial to another. Some information is bypassed or filtered out by the brain as not necessary for survival. Other information causes extreme reactions of fight or flight, or sexual arousal, both of which are necessary for survival (especially the latter!). Even our bodies are made up of information in the form of DNA and genetic coding that influences our physical development.

Though we could go on and on about the various aspects of information in relation to physics and entropy, systems theory, technologically mediated information, semiotics, and abstraction, our focus in this book is information in the form of knowledge, wisdom, and truth, and how it gets from there to here.

Scientific knowledge and understanding, spiritual and religious wisdom, life truths and creative ideas and concepts always existed, albeit not in the complex forms they do in today's web-linked, viral world. Back in ancient times, what people knew and experienced had outlets that we might think of today as crude and ineffective—and yet, we got the messages, and are in the process of trying to interpret them. Ancient art, myth, stories, lore and legend, buildings and architecture, symbols and archetypes, all served as fodder for the transmission methods of the times, and they did work, because today we revel in the discovery of what those myths and legends and symbols and fodder meant, and how they fit into the structure of modern knowledge.

So here's the thing. Back in the day, without aid of high-speed gadgets and viral videos, how did information get from one place to another? We might start by looking at how things go viral in a natural sense, minus the gadgetry.

Let's start with the obvious.

Viva voce is Latin for "by word of mouth." Passing on information by word of mouth, from person to person, is at heart our most basic form of communication as human beings. Along with writing, which came later, we talk. We tell. We describe and convey using words. Cultural and religious tradition is passed down orally. History is passed down orally, in speech and story-telling. Oral tradition is our way of recording and communicating the history of our species for all of posterity. In *Oral Tradition as History,* author Jan Vansina describes it as "verbal messages which are reported statements from the past beyond the present generation." These messages can be spoken, sung, or played along with musical instruments, and must have been passed down at least one generation.

Oral history may involve the passing of personal information, or even societal information from one generation to the next. This form of historical documentation, though effective, often leaves much to be desired because of the possibility of misinformation, disinformation, and even rumor, gaining a foothold in the passing of truth and fact—not to mention the fact that so much of our oral tradition involves actual story-telling and embellishment in which we must weed out the fact from the fiction. Sometimes we even speak in symbols and images that must be interpreted, which leaves the truth open to all kinds of error, not to mention the personal spin those carrying on the oral tradition often put on what they were conveying and transmitting.

But long before we figured out how to scratch out symbols and images on rocks, pick up a pen and put it to paper, and fire up a tablet and get on the Web, we talked it out.

But the way information has been presented and preserved from ancient times is a lot more involved, a lot more complex. It is, at heart, linked intrinsically with our own evolution as a species.

Cultural Evolution

In the fields of anthropology and archeology, cultural evolution presents a theory by which cultures change and replicate in a similar vein to that of genetic evolution. Cultural evolution is an offshoot of the Darwinian evolutionary theory, and examines how cultures are not just influenced by their environment and biology, but by social factors as well.

The theory was developed in the 19th century to describe cultural inheritance of habits and knowledge and behavior, and their relationship to social learning structures within a given species. Different species will have different means by which they learn various habits and knowledge, and how they are passed on to offspring. Charles Darwin posited this to natural adaptation and selection that occurred along either vertical lines—from parent to offspring, or oblique transmission—from peers and authority figures. But cultural evolution goes beyond mere natural selection to explain more complex questions as to how learning and information spread and transmit through various cultures, including something called "prestige bias," which states that individuals in a culture will copy ideas and knowledge from those they consider higher up the prestige chain than themselves.

On the other hand, "conformist bias" posits that we learn from imitation with common types, sort of a "birds of a feather stick together" idea, and this can include imitating any given member of a society or group that appears to be engaging in appropriate behavior. This was especially important for social groups entering an entirely new environment, in the same way today that city folk learn from country folk when they move from Manhattan to the Ozarks. We learn by conforming to those we seek out as being common to us, or with whom we hope to blend in with.

For a culture to evolve, or for any social change to occur, which often requires the spread of information to allow for new knowledge and behaviors, there must be an interaction between the individual and the social environment in which he or she is embedded. We might ask which came first—the individual who makes society, or the society that makes the individual—and find evidence for both. Cultural inheritance, Darwin believed, was learned from one generation to the next via an organic transmission using "gemmules," particles found in the body that ended up in the gonads, then transmitted to offspring via conception. The new generation would be carrying cellular "knowledge" of the prior generation via these gemmules, and thus continue the traits and characteristics of the parental line.

Another key figure in the development of cultural evolutionary theory, Herbert Spencer, wrote about his view of how evolutionary thinking helped drive human culture via deductive or *a priori* knowledge. Spencer was a British philosopher and psychologist who actually coined the term *survival of the fittest*. (The actual quote is "The survival of the fittest, which I have here sought to express in mechanical terms, is that which Mr. Darwin has called 'natural selection, or the preservation of favored races in the struggle for life.'") The experiences, he posited, of past generations were somehow imprinted on human minds as deductive reasoning and knowledge independent of experience, which was then passed on to future generations. This knowledge we possess was that of our ancestors and their experiences, imprinted upon the common mind of all. Spencer also advocated the idea of "use-inheritance," by which individuals and cultures adopted habits and behaviors that were originally utilized by their ancestors. Can learned habits be passed down from one generation to the next? Spencer is quoted in Darwin's classic *Descent of Man* that he believed

> the experiences of utility, organized and consolidated through all past generations of the human race, have been producing corresponding modifications, which, by continued transmission and accumulation, have become in us certain faculties of moral intuition, certain emotions corresponding to right and wrong conduct, which have no apparent basis in the individual experience of utility.

The arguments over which theory best explains cultural evolution and the societal transmission of information continues in the halls of academia, among philosophers and anthropologists, archeologists and psychologists alike. But most can agree that there are certain mechanisms at work by which information is passed around, whether from culture to culture, or generation to generation. Or even person to person to person.

Memes and Memetics

In today's fast-paced world of instant communication, the meme rules. Whether it is Facebook, Instagram, or Twitter, our access and availability to information has changed. A meme is an idea or behavior that spreads within a culture from person to person. It can be done very quickly, as in today's linked-up world, or slowly, as in oral tradition and story passed from one generation to another. Or it can be a secret whispered in the ear of the person standing next to you, who then whispers to another, and another, until everyone had heard the secret (although by the time it gets to the last person, it's a completely different secret!).

Chances are good that if you are on the Internet, especially on the many social networking sites, you know what a meme is. To put it simply, a meme is a concept, idea, action, behavior, or even style that spreads within a particular culture via person-to-person interaction.

Memes can spread via writing, art, rituals, and anything that can be repeated or imitated by someone else. The word *meme* comes from the Ancient Greek *mimeisthai,* "to imitate," and was actually coined by Richard Dawkins, a British evolutionary biologist and ethologist in his 1976 book, *The Selfish Gene,* although references to the idea of the "mneme" as a unit of cultural transmission of experiences was discussed in an earlier 1904 book, *Die Mneme,* by German biologist Richard Semon.

Dawkins, a noted atheist and author of *The God Delusion,* popularized the idea of the gene as the principal unit of selection in evolution. In *The Selfish Gene,* he wrote that a meme was a "cultural replicator" that could be viewed as a unit with the ability to copy or duplicate itself, and that all life evolved from the "differential survival of replicating entities." Ideas, beliefs, catch phrases, and even gestures could be copied via linguistic communication and inference from a person to a person. Ideas, then, which are information, could be thought of as actual entities that hop from one mind to another and make copies as they go, spreading like a mental virus. These would, of course, do so at different rates and speeds, depending on the cultural environment, and eventually might spread beyond one culture to another nearby.

In the same way genes replicate, ideas might do so. Memes therefore can be thought of as the behavioral genes. Dawkins had a lot of skeptics and even scholars who felt he was ignoring the fact that genes are part of their environment, working together. One gene alone does not survival make. But Dawkins strongly supported the idea that for each individual gene, all other genes are a part of its adapted environment. In the same fashion, one meme alone does not a culture make, but memes serve as one driver of ideas within a system.

Memetics is the theory of memes as a driver of evolutionary biology, although it is only one theory. There are issues with memetics being a sole cause of how a culture embraces and transmits ideas and information, and detractors do state that because not all ideas spread through populations in the same manner, not all ideas can be considered replicators, and therefore memes. Another argument posits that cultural units, or memes, do not form lineages the way genes do. For example, a new copy of a gene can be traced back to a single parent, but one cannot trace a single idea as clearly and cleanly back to a single original source.

Ideas do spread through various means of exposure, and many are in fact reproduced again and again until they become a cultural "norm," but they are not necessarily copied from one person to another. One way to look at these differences would be the world of baking and cooking. Take a recipe, and pass it on to a hundred people. Those one hundred people may or may not follow that recipe to a T, and there will be some results that are absolute duplicates, and others that are close calls. Yet the initial idea, or information, remains somewhat intact.

Spread a recipe through several generations and that intact structure may become less and less formal, as people try this or tweak that, yet all the while still staying somewhat true to the original recipe.

Information that pertains to life in the form of genes can be transmitted in two ways: either vertically, from parent to child via genetic replication, or horizontally via the introduction of viruses and so forth. This can also apply to memetics and ideas that spread through generations from parents to offspring, and like viruses through populations, effecting and infecting each person that comes in contact with the idea. Thus, the same drivers in genetics are found present when it comes to memes and ideas.

Mind Viruses

Aaron Lynch, an American author and former engineering physicist at Fermilab, with an educational background in mathematics and philosophy, wrote a seminal book titled *Thought Contagion: How Belief*

Spreads Through Society, in which he documented his theoretical and mathematical models of idea transmission, many of which had been previously published in the scholarly *Journal of Ideas.* Lynch posited that ideas were information that was encoded in the human neurons or in other media, but could also take on new intentional meanings and contagious properties as they evolved, even becoming new belief sets. This included erroneous beliefs and misinformation as well, leading Lynch to state, "People don't learn from each other's mistakes. They learn each other's mistakes." Ideas, therefore, were both embedded and evolving, but did not have a "consciousness" of their own and were driven by things such as fads, trends, mass hysteria, even copycat crimes, and violence—even mob rule mentality.

Interestingly, Lynch put forth seven key patterns of meme/idea transmission that described thought contagion:

1. Quantity of Parenthood—Ideas that influence the number of children a person has. Ideas that encourage higher birth rate will replicate faster than those that discourage it.

2. Efficiency of Parenthood—Ideas that increase the proportion of children who will adopt their parents' ideas.

3. Proselytic—Ideas generally passed to others beyond one's own children, as in religious and political movements, which spread more rapidly horizontally in populations than they do from parent to child.

4. Preservational—Ideas that influence those who continue to believe them for long periods of time, as in traditions. These ideas are hard to abandon or replace.

5. Adversative—Ideas that influence those that hold them to attack, or sabotage competing ideas. Replication gives an advantage to the meme when it encourages aggression against other memes.

6. Cognitive—Ideas perceived as reasonable, convincing, and cogent by most of the population who encounter them. Dependent upon ideas and traits already widely held in a population, thus spreading more passively than other meme types.

7. Motivational—Ideas that people accept and adopt because of some self-interest benefit.

In *Virus of the Mind: The New Science of the Meme,* author Richard Brodie (who, by the way, was the original author of Microsoft Word) writes about the virus-like quality of memes and the spread of ideas, stating that memes influence our behavior in a variety of ways and that, like the gene pool we evolve from, make up a "meme pool." Brodie writes, "Memes spread by influencing people's minds, and thus their behavior, so that eventually someone gets infected with the meme. If a meme is in your mind, it can greatly or subtly influence your behavior." He categorizes memes as follows:

1. Distinction memes—These help us categorize and describe our universe by labeling them.

2. Strategy memes—These are described as "floating rule of thumb that tells you what to do when you come across an applicable situation in order to achieve some desired result."

3. Association memes—These link two or more memes in the mind (for example, the idea of "baseball, hot dogs, apple pie, and Chevrolet" as an advertising meme for the American lifestyle).

We also have peer pressure, personal programming, and instinct and natural programming to deal with, and Brodie suggests we are moving out of an old paradigm of cultural evolution based upon innovation and conquest and into a new one based upon memetics and viruses of the mind: "Our minds excel at both copying information and following instructions.... Remember the four characteristics of a virus: penetration, copying, possibly issuing instructions, and spreading." This, Brodie writes, is how viruses of the mind take hold on populations, whether fashion trends or religious cults. And, not all memes have to even be factual or truthful, as we know from the spread of urban legends, myth, superstition, and rumor.

Religious beliefs seem most susceptible to this virus of the mind behavior. Adding the role of ritual may be even more effective at transmitting the belief system, according to Joseph Henrich, in his interview with *Edge* ("How Culture Drove Human Evolution"). Henrich states: "If you break down rituals common in many religions, they put the words in the mouths of a prestigious member of the group, someone everyone respects. That makes it more likely to transmit and be believed." Things like animal sacrifice and the giving of large amounts of money during a ritual add to that influence as "credibility-enhancing displays" that appear as a demonstration of true belief, and are therefore more likely to be adopted by those observers as their own belief.

Richard Brodie adds in *Virus of the Mind* that because fear and survival were so critical to our ancestors, many myths and religions include some type of threat of retribution from the Gods, warning the populace of the dangers of doing forbidden things. This is a great method of mind control involving memes, because those involving danger are the ones we most pay attention to. Brodie states, "As oral traditions developed, our brains were set up to amplify the dangers and give them greater significance than the rest."

Anti-Memes

Not everyone sings the praises of memes and memetics. In a *Psychology Today* article titled "Hot Thought: Why Memes Are a Bad Idea," Paul Thagard puts forth the argument that variation, selection, and transmission in minds and cultures is not the same as it is in genetic passing on of information. He suggests that cultural generation of ideas is more goal-oriented than genetic mutation, and that the selection of ideas involves the use of both emotion and intellectual criteria, and not just the survival-based issues of genetics. Transmission of ideas is more rapid and widespread in a culture, as well, unlike the slow progression of genetic adaption and transmission. An idea can spread through a population of millions in a matter of days, not generations.

Philosophical differences aside, information often manages to work its way through environments and populations, often with stunning speed. One recent theory of cultural evolution take into account things like "conformation bias," which is the tendency of individuals and groups to buy into beliefs they feel are the most commonly adhered to or represented in a populace. Proposed by anthropologist and professor of psychology and economics Joseph Heinrich, and anthropologist and coauthor of *How Humans Evolved* Robert Boyd, conformation bias suggests that what everyone else believes, others tend to go along with, and those beliefs get transmitted in a snowball effect, influencing more and more people who may have chosen not to think for themselves. What is commonly held to be "truth" in one generation may be passed on to future generations, as are traditions and beliefs, with room for error, but the core truths remain.

Henrich and Boyd argue that a workable evolutionary theory rarely works through just the idea of genuine copying, that there are a number of "attractors" or manners of thinking that populations adopt in light of certain environmental and external stimuli. Thus you can have differential success in emulation of a particular cultural model without having to resort to exact copying, as in memes. (In a later chapter, we will look at the influence of memes on popular culture today.)

Henrich champions the idea that cultural and biological evolution must be looked at together, not as separate entities in the course of overall evolution. Obviously, we have changed both genetically and behaviorally since the dawn of humanity. We are not still living in caves and hunting with spears. New ways of doing things and new ways of thinking have been as much a part of our evolution as developing less-hairy bodies and standing up straighter when we walk.

Though all of this can be confusing, the goal is to determine not just how we humans evolved, but how our cultures did as well, and how we learned and acquired information over time, either from our ancestors or from our own novel experiences. We are not talking just about instinctual behaviors, which are learned as critical to species survival, and then passed on through the genetic line. We are talking about behaviors and beliefs that have nothing to do with survival, or instinct, yet seem to get passed along in the same mysterious way.

We might get an idea of how information spread in ancient times by looking at how it spreads today, in a theoretical sense at least. Other than memes, we could be dealing with:

Mental Networks

The spread of information has often been described like a computer network, with minds interlinked and able to pass on ideas within the network in a similar structure. There is actually something called "network science" that studies sociology, medicine, and statistics to determine how everything from products to behavior to even sneezes and yawns are contagious. In an interview for *Fast Company*, Drake Baer talked to Harvard Medical School professor Nicholas Christakis about the science of networks.

"Things don't just diffuse in human populations at random. They actually diffuse through networks," Christakis states. Our networks are the relationship webs we have with friends, colleagues, and family, and the more central we are to that network, the more connections we have to others, and the more access to ideas and information.

But just as those central to a network are at higher exposure of ideas and memes that are novel and untested, it doesn't always put us at an advantage. Being at the center of the network increases your risk, Christakis says, of also being infected with bad information and ideas, and adopting them as your own. As with the transmission of memes, networks operate along vertical lines of influence, as well as horizontal, and if you have more relationships across the network, you have more access to ideas and information from the collective.

Diffusion

One theory in particular attempts to explain how new ideas and innovations, especially those involving technology, spread throughout a populace. The theory of diffusion, first posited by sociologist Everett Rogers in his 1962 book, *Diffusion of Innovations,* posits that social systems drive or dictate the successful adoption of a new idea or technology, as well as whether or not that idea is sustained over time. Rogers looked at more than 500 studies involving diffusion and researched the topic in the fields of anthropology and sociology, most notable rural sociology, which was his expertise.

Rogers states that an idea or innovation must be created, then communicated, then given enough processing time to be adopted by enough members of a social system to become saturated, or reach critical mass. The social system is critical, as without an idea catching on, there can be no saturation point where the idea or technology becomes a widely accepted part of life and culture. What is interesting was Rogers's finding that people don't evaluate a new idea or innovation on the basis of scientific studies of its consequences. Rather, they focus on "a subjective evaluation of an innovation that is conveyed to them from other individuals like themselves."

Therefore, a more perception-oriented decision is involved in order for a new innovation to take hold and reach critical mass. As with something you might buy—a car or a new fridge, for example—most people were found to take the advice of a friend over what they read or researched about which product is best.

So, an individual's social system often holds more weight as to what information will be adopted, accepted, and passed on to future generations than hard science or factual research. Again, look at religious beliefs, superstitions, and urban legends, and one can easily see how word of mouth from a "trusted" source holds more weight than facts! This may explain the trend of viral videos and images, even the downloading of music today, which can be manipulated by "false downloads" to appear to be more popular than it really is, thus resulting in even more "real downloads." One has to wonder if this also applies to best-seller lists of books and whether readers are being swayed to buy a book, or even see a movie, for that matter, that is really not selling well at all—all the more powerful and influential if that suggestion comes from a friend.

This kind of diffusion may also apply to rumor and gossip, and why we tend to put more weight on what we are told by friends, even if it has no truth behind it, or why people side with conspiracy theorists more so than their own government, because of an identification with the conspiracy folks as being "victims of the Man," even if the conspiracy crowd has no fact to back up their own claims. (More on this later.)

Tipping Points

Like critical mass, we have tipping points.

Think about a scale. You put an equal amount of rocks on both sides to keep it in balance, but put more rocks on one side and eventually the scale tips. A "tipping point" is a sociological term for that particular point in time when a large group adopts a particular practice, idea, or behavior, and changes/alters its behavior accordingly. Tipping points can occur with fashion trends, political revolutions, or product popularity, and they occur when a critical mass of adoption is achieved. It's a point of no return, during which something that was not even a part of the norm before is now increasing so rapidly within the group as to be considered epidemic. Tipping points are similar to the domino effect, viral contagion, information cascade, and even chaos theory, all of which offer a similar concept of information/ideas reaching critical mass.

A number of sociologists and researchers have put forth tipping point models for collective behavior, including a Nobel Prize winner in 1972: Thomas Schelling, a distinguished professor of economics at the University of Maryland who received the prize in Economic Science. But it was British-Canadian journalist Malcolm Gladwell who created a tipping point for tipping points with his seminal book *The Tipping Point: How Little Things Make a Big Difference.* Published in 2000, *The Tipping Point* introduced a sociological concept to a wide enough audience that now the phrase is often associated with Gladwell and his work.

Gladwell describes a tipping point as the moment critical mass is achieved, or the "boiling point" that occurs when our lives are changed by a new idea. He cites three rules as the agents of change driving social epidemics:

1. The "Law of the Few" or 80/20 Principle—Most of the work will be done by the fewest participants. In this case, approximately at a ratio of 80 to 20. The participants possess rare skills as connectors, mavens, or salesmen. Connectors are those who know a lot of people within a social system, and make connections and introductions of others. Gladwell equates connectors to a computer network hub, as these people have a wide variety of contacts in all social circles and possess a knack for

making new friendships and connections. Next are the mavens, who specialize in a certain type of information and are the people we turn to for specific knowledge. These are the people who start "word of mouth epidemics"; Gladwell calls them "information brokers." Last are the salesmen, who persuade others to do something or buy something with their negotiation skills. These three types of people drive tipping points within a social system.

2. The Stickiness Factor—An idea or content must be "sticky" or memorable in order to achieve critical mass with a populace. Impact comes from a higher stickiness factor.

3. Context—A social epidemic must have identifiable context for a vast number of people in order for them to adopt it as a part of their behavior. Because we are strongly influenced by our environment, a social tipping point must be relevant in contest to the "conditions and circumstances of the times and places in which they occur."

In an interview on his Website (Gladwell.com), Malcolm Gladwell equates tipping points to outbreaks of diseases: "Why is word of mouth so powerful? What makes TV shows like Sesame Street so good at teaching kids how to read? I think the answer to all those questions is the same. It's that ideas and behavior and messages and products sometimes behave just like outbreaks of infectious disease. They are social epidemics."

Once Gladwell saw the pattern of outbreak, he saw it everywhere in the spread of ideas and new products and human behaviors. "This isn't just a metaphor, in other worlds. I'm talking about a very literal analogy. One of the things I explore in the book is that ideas can be contagious in exactly the same way that a virus is." Gladwell finds some similarities with memes, but argues that memes are difficult to pin down in terms of why they become so contagious. But, he believes that people can actually start "positive epidemics" of their own, because they require little input to get started, can spread very quickly (especially in this day and age), and can reach a large number of people in the process. Of course, this can be done with negative social epidemics as well, something we tackle in a later chapter.

Mostly, to Gladwell, it's about understanding how and why major changes often happen quickly in our world, and how we can decode that confusing change more easily by understanding the patterns of tipping points.

Jumping Jesus, Multiple Discovery, Mass Consciousness, and a Hundred Monkeys

Some of the more whimsical concepts of multiple discovery, or the fast spread of ideas from culture to culture, include the Hundredth Monkey Effect, which refers to a sudden and spontaneous leap of knowledge or consciousness when critical mass or a tipping point is achieved. This can even occur across cultural boundaries. The term comes from a book, *Lifetide* by Dr. Lyall Watson, PhD, an ethologist working at the London Zoo. Watson was researching and writing about the work of Japanese primatologists in the 1960s involving macaques. According to Watson's book, one macaque taught another how to wash sweet potatoes, and that macaque taught another, and so on and so on until the entire island they inhabited were adopting the behavior. But where the Hundredth Monkey Effect occurred was the moment when monkeys on other islands suddenly began washing potatoes! These monkeys had no visible means of communication with the original potato-washers, so how then could they suddenly adopt such a behavior? Was it some type of psychic communication via mass consciousness? Telepathic knowledge on behalf of the primate community? Or perhaps did the monkeys on the new islands just coincidentally figure out that washed potatoes were better to eat than dirty ones?

Skeptics jumped down Watson's throat, citing research on behalf of others who knew nothing of this spontaneous spread of behavior, including the comment by Watson's own colleague, Masao Kawai, a senior researcher on the original macaque project, who claimed in an interview with *Skeptical Inquirer* in 1996 that he wasn't aware of any skills "that propagated more rapidly than would be expected by normal, individual, pre-cultural propagation."

Still, the idea of multiple discovery, a term used by historians and sociologists to describe multiple independent discoveries, does happen, in science, art, and knowledge, and is often linked to memetics, cultural evolution, and evolutionary epistemology, which applies concepts of biological evolution to the spread of human knowledge culturally.

But can we ascribe this to some mystical-sounding implicate mass consciousness or some field of information that is accessible to everyone and anyone at any given time, containing within it all ideas and knowledge? We will tackle that big issue later. Yet even Carl Jung felt there were two ways that human beings could transmit information to each other. One was by genetic transmission, and the other was by some other type of communication, including cultural, mythological, and symbolic. Jung believed that archetypes, or specific mental patterns of information that exist within all human minds and consciousness, were genetically transmitted information, as well as genetically inherited. The powerful symbolism of archetypes was to be understood on a level of communication that wasn't obvious, but was still a part of the psyche. In fact, to Jung, contact with archetypes led to both the rise of myth and religion.

The Ghost in Our Genes
By Lorraine Evans

There can be no doubt that the world of our ancient ancestors has shaped our modern modular mind. Yet the scarcity of hard evidence from prehistoric times, especially with regards to physical changes in the brain, makes it impossible to delve inside the minds of our forbearers to extract information. Psychologists and cognitive archaeologists have tried their best to provide an insight into this conundrum and have proposed varied hypotheses, which include "cognitive fluidity," a developmental process whereby our prehistoric ancestors acquired the skills to use artifacts to store and transmit information; a "mythic" culture, which involved the ability to construct conceptual models in the form of material symbolism, closely associated with the evolution of language; and the rise of a human consciousness, which can best be described as a "global database that integrates the output of modular processes." Valiant though these efforts may be, it is guesswork at best. But what if our ancient ancestors had indeed left some residual clues in our genetic code? What if experts could dig into the brain, like an archaeologist, and uncover the history and meaning of our ancient past?

It has long been known that our physical appearance, together with certain diseases and biological disorders, is determined by our parents' genetic material, their DNA. The conventional viewpoint argues that a person's DNA sequence acts as genetic blueprint for development, it carries only heritable information, and nothing an individual does in his or her lifetime can be biologically passed onto their respective offspring. In spite of this perceived notion recent studies from around the world are now challenging this perspective and suggest that our inherent encoded DNA may affect every aspect of our lives. Although controversial within the scientific community,

some have even called it "heresy"; a number of scientists are now
questioning the accepted view of the DNA sequence and believe
that our individual genes are shaped, in part, by our ancestors' life
experience. As the Rockefeller University molecular biologist C. David
Allis stated, "It has really been a watershed in understanding that
there is something beyond the genome."

This new avenue of scientific research is referred to as
"epigenetics," literally meaning "on top of genetics," and is the
study of how individual gene switches can be activated or deactivated
by life experience and environment, together with the appearance
of individual genes through the distribution of DNA. In effect, a
chemical tag, known as an epigenetic mark, is attached to the DNA
that subsequently tells a cell to use or ignore that particular gene.
These tags act as a kind of cellular memory. As cells grow and divide,
cellular machinery faithfully copies these epigenetic tags alongside the
DNA. This is especially important during embryonic development, as
past experiences inform future choices. Epigenetic tags give the cell
a way to "remember" long-term what its genes should be doing and
allows cells to remember their past experiences long after the signals
fade away.

An example of such research was made public a short time ago
by Professor Wolf Reik, from the Babraham Institute in Cambridge,
who has spent years studying this hidden genetic world. Working
specifically with rodents he found that by manipulating the embryos
was enough to activate such epigenetic "switches" to turn the
genes on or off. Moreover, he also discovered that the "switches"
themselves could be passed down from one generation to the next,
signifying that a "memory" of an event could similarly be inherited.
Other tantalizing evidence, from a remote town in northern Sweden,
found that by analyzing the parish records of births and deaths and
accompanying harvest data it revealed that famines experienced by

...✦ *Get It* ✦...

...an overwhelming genetic effect on subsequent
...d like to make it clear that this is the not the first
...has been put forward. Before Charles Darwin had
...ciples of natural selection in *On the Origin of Species,*
...y French naturalist, Jean–Baptiste Lamarck, had already
propose... .ry different theory of evolution, whereby organisms could
pass on traits they had acquired over their lifetime via their genetic
makeup. Ridiculed after Darwinism took hold, by applying today's
notion of epigenetics, it appears that the Frenchman may have been
onto something after all.

The notion of hidden DNA memories is also not a new one.
During the 1960s and 1970s a number of medical studies were carried
out utilizing isolation tanks and chemical stimulants to supposedly
unlock the genetic mind. The researchers claimed they had successfully
gained access to both DNA memories and experiences alike, although
such research has now been discounted due to the lack of reliable
scientific data it produced. All the same these studies did spawn a rather
intriguing Hollywood film in 1988 entitled *Altered States,* whereby a
research scientist, played by William Hurt, relives various experiences
of his ancestors via his consciousness and genetic origins. Equally the
ideas expressed in epigenetics could also be applied to those of past
life regression and the concept of "déjà vu." Rather than dismissed as
mere fanciful folly by the scientific fraternity, unlike before I believe
epigenetics offers a tangible quantifiable method of recording such
experiences within a systematic and learned framework.

The field of epigenetics is now at the forefront of a paradigm
shift in scientific thinking and many other fields of academic study
are striving to keep pace. New research at the Weizmann Institute
of Science, in Israel, has recently come to light, which complements
those working in epigenetics. Instead of focusing on DNA sequencing,
scientists here have been examining the neurological patterns within

the brain and have discovered that spontaneous waves of activity bear the imprints of earlier events long after the experience has taken place. In short, it is claimed that the pattern of resting brain waves may represent "archives" for earlier experiences. Let me explain further. When a person is resting with closed eyes, with no visual stimuli, the normal bursts of nerve cell activity associated with incoming information are replaced by ultra-slow patterns of neuronal activity. These patterns then travel in a highly organized manner throughout the brain cortex, its outer layer. It is thought that past experiences would thus be incorporated into the network between the nerve cells within this cortex. This research suggests that spontaneously emerging brain patterns could be used as a "mapping tool" for unearthing cognitive events from an individual's past.

So what does this new innovative research have to do with the concept of viral mythology? Evidently if ancient human experience can be passed through the generations via our genetic blueprint, it opens up a world of possibilities when trying to solve many of the questions asked in this book. Epigenetic inheritance adds another dimension to the modern picture of evolution whereby the secrets of the ancient world, once thought lost, could conceivably be retrieved. Today those at the forefront of epigenetic study focus their attention upon the treatment of sickness and disease. A noble cause I hasten to add.

Yet personally I believe by adopting a multi-disciplinary approach, i.e. gene inheritance combined with brain wave mapping, the mysteries of our archaic past could one day be unlocked. It is a path I intend to follow for my own doctoral research and I am hopeful that many of you who are reading this may wish to accompany me on this extraordinary journey into the unknown.

Lorraine Evans is a Research Fellow in Egyptology and Ancient History at the IIPSGP and is currently studying for her PhD on the

*ancient Egyptian concept of Maat. She is author of the best-selling
book* Kingdom of the Ark, *examining the links between Egypt and
Ireland, together with* Warrior Women of Northern Europe *and* Murder
at Medinet Habu—A Heritage Tour Guide. *Lorraine is regarded as
a groundbreaking academic researcher, writer, and broadcaster. Her
research skills are often in demand and comprise the best-selling books*
Tutankhamun: The Exodus Theory, The Tutankhamun Deception,
Act of God, Moses the Legacy, *and* Gods of Eden, *among others. She
has worked as an academic advisor on many internationally acclaimed
TV documentaries, including* Secrets of the Dead, The Tutankhamun
Deception, Gladiatrix, *and* The Soaring Stones *(The History Channel),
and has served on a number of archaeology committees including the
Institute of Field Archaeologists, the Museology Committee, Egyptian
Museum Cairo (FEMC), and Lanista Ancient Warfare Academy, to
name but a few.*

But before we tackle those two realms, we need to point out that
although we've been talking a lot about how information is spread and
transmitted today, these same theories and concepts could have easily
been at work in ancient cultures, along with other theories we will dig
into a bit later. The way information spreads always begins with the
person spreading it, and how he or she chooses to do that does depend
on the times, and the means at hand. But in the end, we know that
ideas catch on like wildfire, like disease, and we are infected with them
on a regular basis. Sometimes those ideas are hidden within a greater
context, or presented to us in something other than words. Sometimes
ideas fail to reach a tipping point and are relegated to memory or nostalgia. And sometimes, they stick for good and become a part of who
we are as human beings.

Sometimes, ideas and innovations spread so quickly our minds boggle. Many theories point to an exponential increase in the amount of novelty and new information we are being bombarded with, and how it might affect our brain's capacity and ability to process it. One such humorous idea is the Jumping Jesus Phenomenon created by Robert Anton Wilson as part of a long lecture he gave in 1986 titled "The Acceleration of Knowledge." Wilson proposed that we use a "Jesus" as a new measurement to comprise the sum of known scientific fact starting from the year 1 CE. To arrive at just one "Jesus," then, it took our species between 40,000 and 100,000 years. But since then, each doubling of accumulated information happens in an increasingly shorter period of time, so that it would take less and less time to reach more and more "Jesus" units. Wilson was being comedic, but many researchers took his theory and developed it into their own novelty theories about how information is doubling exponentially faster, leading to a point of "singularity" possibly, when we will suddenly and spontaneously know everything all at once!

By the way, the term *Jumping Jesus* refers possibly to the use of "Jesus on a pogo stick" as a mild curse or exclamation—but then can we really count on the accuracy of that information? And that is the problem we face: more and more information coming at us, from more and more sources, not all of them based upon solid fact or certainty, and we are left trying to sort truth from rumor, wisdom from wackiness, knowledge from complete and utter BS.

While we are looking for the drivers and mechanisms by which information gets transmitted throughout time, from one person to another person, or one culture to another culture, we cannot ignore the fact that very often information isn't passed on in direct ideas, behaviors, styles, or gestures. In fact, sometimes information is transmitted not as ideas at all, but as stories, and that the truth can only be found when, and only when, we read between the lines.

Every Picture Tells a Story (Don't It?): Image, Art, and Symbol

I know of no other group of artists, be they paint-
ers, architects or composers, who have not gone
into their own pasts, keen to gather all that had a
bearing on their art.
  —Ruth Sawyer, *The Way of the Storyteller*

The earliest forms of story-telling were basically oral, either spoken or sung, and later art in the form of symbols and images meant to convey information on cave walls, rocks, dirt, sand, clay, pottery, stone tablets, animal skins, parchment, and even in the trunks of trees. Nature provided both easel and drawing implement with crude stones and even dyes that acted like paints—primitive crayon art, if you will. Even the paint used on the bodies of various tribal and indigenous peoples served to tell a story, as these earliest forms of tattoos were truly symbolic.

Visual Stories

Visual story-telling has been around as long as 300,000–700,000 (the age is still disputed) years ago, with the crude petroglyphs discovered in the Auditorium Cave and Daraki-Chattan Cave of the ancient quartzite Bhimbetka caves in India, and 40,000 years ago, when pigment was used to create painted images on the walls of caves in Europe, most notably in Spain and France. The oldest cave paintings to date have been found on the walls of the Cave of Altamira in Santander, Spain, dating back some 40,000 years to the Aurignacian period. These Paleolithic cave paintings are found throughout an 11-site subterranean system along Spain's Cantabrian seacoast. The oldest paintings are in the El Castillo, which some archeologists claim date back to almost 40,800 years ago. If this date is correct—and there is some controversy as always in the often indirect dating methods that are required—then El Castillo would also don the title of oldest known dated cave paintings in the world.

What makes these paintings so special, other than their sheer age, is the possibility that they could have in part been created by Neanderthals, who populated that part of Europe at the same time, along with modern Homo sapiens. Classified as "symbolic art," the images correspond to other recent discoveries of body paint, art objects, and pigments at Neanderthal sites that show our ancient cave men and women weren't as primitive as we might have thought. Neanderthals, in fact, have shown the same type of evolutionary trajectory that our human ancestors emerging from Africa showed, as they progressed toward the use of art.

The oldest cave art at El Castillo is made up of disks, dots, and hand stencils, but there is also plenty of "figurative art" of animals such as horses and bison. It may be a part of what many scientists call the "upper Paleolithic Revolution," or the Late Stone Age, which dates from 50,000 to 100,000 years ago, when we as a species experienced a huge leap forward in agriculture, culture, and communication, as these images may have actually been meant to communicate information to others, possibly even in a ritualistic and religious sense. This revolutionary period led to a marked diversity in artifacts, tools, blades, and weaponry, and, of course, art, which soon led to more complicated and sophisticated carvings and engravings, figurines and petroglyphs, which often were distinct in cultural differences as more complex social groups emerged.

This ancient art was thematic, with images of large wild animals prevailing, usually those species that were able to be hunted and used for food and clothing, but some animals may have been more symbolically depicted for ritual purposes, as in shamanic practices of taking on an animal's power, rather than a "story" of what the hunters brought home for dinner that night.

Humans were not often depicted, perhaps because of religious taboos, although on later figurines and artifacts, women—especially pregnant or nursing women—were often objects of fascination. Nature and fecundity was a popular theme, mirroring what goes on in the wild just as it did in the realm of the human.

Often, the art was more engraved than actually painted with ochre, hematite, and charcoal, some of the favored tools of prehistoric artists, but are still defined as cave paintings.

Other cave art in Africa and Australia depicts flora and fauna, some now extinct. African cave art is more likely to feature humans, and one cave, the Laas Gaa'l in northwestern Somalia, even depicts human animal herders. Australian cave art points to unusual animal species that may have been extinct more than 40,000 years ago and may give us a glimpse far into the past of a world where animals and birds we will never know of existed.

Africa is also home to the first known rock art including one site of thousands of engravings and drawings time lining various climate shifts, animal migrations, and human inhabitation patterns dating back to 6000 BC. Rock art was the natural progression of cave art.

The second oldest known cave art comes from France. Known as the Chauvet-Pont-d'Arc Cave, this is one of the most important prehistoric art sites, and one of the oldest, although again the dating is a bit controversial. In the Chauvet Cave (named after one of the initial French speleologists to explore the cave, Jean-Marie Chauvet, who left a detailed account of the explorations), humans who lived during two time periods, the Aurignacian (30,000–32,000 years ago) and the latter Gravettian (25,000–27,000 years ago), the cave may feature the oldest known human footprints as well. In the cave are a variety of highly detailed depictions of more than a dozen species of animals, some now extinct or rare for other regions at the time, in various forms of inter-action with one another, which served to tell a story about the natu-

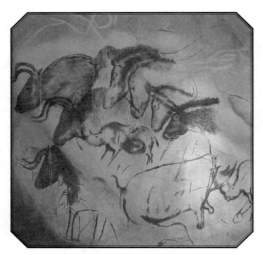

ral world the artists existed in. These artists were not as crude as we might think, and often found a way to smoothen the cave walls by some early form of sanding that allowed for better use of the space. Often, images were actually outlined first, then filled in, and the cave walls themselves added to the dimensional effect by providing various textures.

Figure 2-1: Replica of 31,000-year-old paintings found on the Chauvet Cave.

Scholars have done radio-carbon dating on the cave, which some say date back to the later Early Magdalenian period, although in general the cave art is believed to be far older. Luckily the cave has been cut off from public tourism to best preserve what may have been symbolic imagery used in shamanic and religious "hunting" rituals. (We will discuss this use of symbol and ritual in a later chapter.)

Another fascinating and well-known art-packed cave site is Lascaux in southwestern France, believed to have some of the most sophisticated cave art of the Paleolithic period. Lascaux is really a series of inter-connected caves depicting more than 2,000 figures of everything from horse to bison to mammoths, ibex, deer, lions, wolves, and even a human, dating all the way back to 15,000 BC. The cave paintings were allegedly discovered in 1949 by a group of French children, have since become among the most critical finds in the field of primitive art, and are said to be in mural form as they tell a story of hunting rituals and practices of the day. Folklorists have been said to find a narrative in the mural-like depiction, according to Dr. Michael Lockett in *The Basics of Storytelling.* Lockett writes, "It is believed that the cave was used for the performance of hunting and magical rituals. Whatever its purpose, it serves as evidence that stories and storytelling have been around for a long, long time!"

Lascaux is also rich with engravings and even abstract designs created most likely by the light of torches and lamps filled with animal fat. The artists of Lascaux, like those of all caves throughout history, chose these hidden, dark places to describe and convey their interpretation and perception of the world they lived in, which was focused then on survival and thus gave special importance to the animals that provided the means of survival for the species. But because of the threats of tourists and exposure to elements, the Lascaux Cave and others are being replicated for visitors to avoid contamination of the original sites, which are now only open on a very limited basis to qualified researchers.

Needless to say, cave paintings and art exists at various historical intervals all over the world and are often designated as World Heritage Sites by UNESCO, the United Nations Educational, Scientific and Cultural Organization. Many of the caves mirror those of their region, but some stand out, such as the Edakkal in Kerala, India, which depicts actual images of tribal chieftains and queens. Dating back approximately 7,000–8,000 years, the imagery is described less as art and more as "pictorial writings" as history progresses toward the prominence of the written word.

North American Cave Art

In the North American region, Native American cave pictographs are found all over the continent that depict humans often in head-dresses, along with animals and other often geometrical symbols, dating back to thousands of years ago. The Chumash Indians are known for the numerous cave paintings attributed to their culture throughout the Southern California region. Researchers argue over whether the images depicted are dreams, visions, or even astronomical symbols, and even Chumash elders have had a difficult time interpreting the art of their ancient elders, which they see as not just links to their past, but stories of their heritage.

One of the oldest known cave art sites in America dates back a good 6,000 years. One wouldn't expect the Cumberland Plateau of Tennessee to hold such a unique part of history, but archeologists have recently discovered the oldest cave and rock art scattered in caves around the area that spans from the Kentucky border down into northern Alabama. But it is in Tennessee that the oldest image, a painting of a hunter, was dated as 6,000 years old, which would make it the oldest of its kind in the States. These caves are part of what is called a "dark-zone" of cave sites east of the Mississippi, and archeologists are discovering new caves all the time. A dark-zone site is a location where the natives who created the artwork did so at personal risk, underground in the darkness, most likely only lit by their own torches or crude lamps. Twilight-zone sites, on the other hand, cover cave mouths and entrances that were able to maintain diffuse sunlight.

Most of the images are dated between 500 and 900 years ago, but the oldest images come from locales in the middle of Tennessee, including those on the Cumberland Plateau, which is riddled with various types of caves, including pit caves, dome caves, and the wider tourist caves. The glyphs dating back about 800 years appeared to belong to the Mississippian people, ancestors to today's Southeastern and Midwestern tribes, and appeared to be of the category "Southeastern Ceremonial Complex—SECC," which was a part of a little understood religious movement that swept the Eastern part of the continent in 1200 AD.

In a June 2013 interview with CNN's Matt Smith titled "Ancient Tennessee Cave Paintings Show Deep Thinking by Natives," University of Tennessee anthropologist Jan Simek commented on the enormous scale of the painting complex of caves: "There is a cosmology being expressed...and one of the things we're trying to suggest is the composition has an enormous scale." The art depicted throughout the 94 sites were very thematic. Above-ground works at 44 of the sites were done mostly in red that may have represented life and the dramatic sky of the spring and summer months, which would have been more impactful from these south- and west-facing locations. Images were found possibly suggesting an "upper world" of weather, sky, and starry influences, with locations nearer the surface focusing more on "middle world" people, plant, and animal life. In many of the images, humans are portrayed doing things and doing, as Simek describes, "otherworldly" kinds of things, which parallels the Native American belief that caves are places where the boundary between the natural world and the spirit world are thinner and can be crossed.

Anthropomorphism is a popular theme in these caves, first appearing during the Archaic period, and showing human figures with clearly animal or birdlike qualities such as wings or exaggeratedly long fingers and horns.

According to Simek, "The art sites, predominately found in caves, feature otherworldly characters, supernatural serpents and dogs that accompanied dead humans on the path of souls." This imagery is painted in black and represents a much deeper symbology than just which animals were to be hunted for dinner that night. These mysterious creatures are described as mythical and representative of Native American beliefs, and are much more elaborate than the more crudely carved or drawn imagery of hunting rituals. Glyphs found in the Mud Glyph Cave in particular are the most detailed and elaborate, with human imagery that speaks of ceremonial actions such as flying, shape shifting, and reaching through rock surfaces, according to Nicholas Herrmann, also a part of the scientific research group studying the preserved artworks of the Cumberland Plateau.

Another common symbol found throughout the caves is the circle, which in the Dunbar Cave is shown in the form of rayed circles, circles with crosses inside, and alongside concentric circle pictographs. Interestingly, some of the initially discovered images even appeared to have been ritualistically mutilated, as in stabbed with a stick.

The oldest of the imagery features humans alongside wild dogs such as wolves and jackals, humans portrayed with tools, serpents and beastly creatures, and sometimes more celestial imagery that suggests a spiritual nature for the drawings, rather than purely informational. Simek stated, "The discoveries tell us that prehistoric people in the Cumberland Plateau used this rather distinctive upland environment for a variety of purposes and that religion was part of that broader sense of place."

Ancient Taggers and Old School Graffiti

Who would have thought the art of graffiti dated back to ancient Egypt, Rome, and Greece? What we today consider vandalism and defacing public property with gang tags and mural art out of a spray can actually has its origins in times long before the advent of spray paint.

The word *graffiti* itself comes from the Greek *graphein*, meaning "to write," and the Italian *graffiato*, or "to scratch," and is a technique that was often used on the walls of ancient temples, sepulchers, ruin stones, and columns. The earliest known example of ancient graffiti comes to us from the eighth century BC. Discovered in a tomb in the gulf of Naples, Italy, the graffiti consists of Greek text found on a vessel known as the Nestor Cup. A number of examples of graffiti have been discovered at an excavation near Smyrna in modern-day Turkey, incised or carved on marble, and consisting of everything from board games to prayers, symbols, and offensive and pornographic comments and obscene imagery. This ancient pornography, according to Greek professor Angelos Chaniotis in an interview for *Archeology News Network* (April 19, 2013), was meant to offend and humiliate the opposition during games and battles. These peeks into the daily life of an ancient culture suggest that graffiti was the historical equivalent of cheers and jeers during, say, a football game, with one side attempting to anger or humiliate the other.

Figure 2-2: Second-century pagan graffiti depicting a man worshipping a crucified donkey or mule, with the inscription "Alexamenos respects God," found in the Palatine Hill Museum, Rome, Italy.

Whether in the form of inscribed words or drawings, ancient graffiti was symbolic of the culture and lifestyle of the time, and was just as often serious and sarcastic as it was humorous and witty. Graffiti found at the ancient city of Pompeii is said to include cuss words of the era, as well as love poems, advertisements for local brothels, magical spells, political slogans, curses, and wisdom quotes that provide insight into the history of the region. Ancient graffiti has been found in the Mayan culture, the Norse and Scandinavian cultures, and the British Isles, and suggests that scrawling, carving, and painting on walls was a means of expression just as today's urban culture utilizes.

Primitive Art Categories

If cave walls were nowhere to be found, primitive artists used what was around. Rock art can be broken up into three categories:

1. Petroglyphs are incisions, carvings, and engravings on rock.

2. Petrographs are images drawn or painted on rock.

3. Petroforms are art created with rocks and boulders to form patterns and shapes.

Rock art has been found all over the world, dating back thousands of years and again offered a ready-made canvas for cultural expression. The first rock art traces back to the Neolithic era, before the advent of metalworking led to the Bronze Age and more sophisticated art mediums, and the Iron Age, where writing systems began to appear, spreading from Ancient Egypt to China. As stated earlier, the oldest known petroglyphs have been discovered in the Bhimbetka Caves of India, dating as far back as 300,000–700,000 years. In the Blombos Cave of South Africa, engraved stones have been discovered dating back more than 70,000 years, though the markings were crude grid and cross-hatch patterns.

Many petroglyphs mirrored imagery found on cave art, such as animals and hunting scenes, but others also included humans and even the precursors to writing systems, which began to appear between 7,000 and 9,000 years ago. These precursors were in the forms of pictographs and ideograms.

Pictograms are either pictures or images that represent or resemble a physical object. Using pictures to symbolize something was considered an art form as many of these images were inscribed, carved, and drawn on cave walls and rock arts in Pre-Columbian time.

An ideogram is simply a symbol, picture, or image that represents an idea or concept, rather than an actual physical object.

Ideographic communication and imagery was a precursor to writing systems used in the Bronze Age and is mirrored in the Egyptian hieroglyphs, Sumerian cuneiforms, and Chinese logograms. Before we learned to write with actual words, we wrote with images and symbols that eventually evolved into the alphabet, phonetics, and more sophisticated writing systems.

Some of the oldest recognizable petroglyphs, aside from more crude representations of scratches, cross-hatch marks, and animal shapes, were actual maps and trail guides to nomadic tribes, detailing the presence of water and the type of terrain, as well as possible territorial lines. Later glyphs carried a strong religious and cultural meaning that may have served as a way of passing on information to future generations, somewhat similar to our headstones and grave markers and inscribed historical monuments of today.

Symbols and Spirits

Aboriginal rock art found in Australia dates at least 40,000 years ago, and combines representations of both known animals at the time and mythical creatures that may have been ancient creators that taught the native people what they needed to know about the world around them. Rocks inside well-protected caves and outcroppings may have sheltered Aboriginal tribes and their cave and rock art, much of which is spiritual in nature and symbolizes the creation of the world as understood by the natives.

Aborigines believed the paintings actually contained spiritual powers of the entities and beings that were represented and they went to extreme lengths to revere, protect, and preserve these paintings, often actually repairing damage and touching up images all the way up to modern times. Though again most images were of creatures indigenous to the region, many were also considered "Mimi spirits," located

at the highest points on the rock and walls. These paintings were said to have been artwork of the Mimi, which are thin, delicate, almost stick-figure-like entities that lived in the cracks and nooks of the rocky landscape. The Mimi also taught the natives how to paint, hunt, and create music, and were often depicted in action, dancing, hunting, fighting, and running.

African rock art in the high mountains of Southern Africa features more than 20,000 rock paintings by the Bushmen, known as San, who were the indigenous hunter-gatherer tribe of the region. These paintings, found in caves and overhangs, feature spectacular images of a

Figure 2-3: A Type 1 Pictish stone with incised symbols, found at Dunnichen, Angus, Scotland, an example of Medieval stone art. Image courtesy of Catfish Jim and the Soapdish.

variety of animals drawn in great detail. Some of the oldest rock art, dating from the Upper Paleolithic period, is found in Australia and Africa, and often had great spiritual significance. Some imagery was associated with magical beliefs of the indigenous peoples and was produced during rituals held within the cave sites. Many of these cultures were shamanic in nature and the common themes of bones; skeletal remains and skeletal decorative items spoke to the shamanic belief in death and revival. Other identifying marks on the rock art include different types and shapes of drums, a staple in shamanic rituals and journeying, or even initiation ceremonies.

A recent discovery by a team of University of Colorado researchers, led by Larry Benson, turned up what might be the oldest known petroglyphs in North America. Using high-tech analysis on cuts made into several boulders in western Nevada, these enigmatic petroglyphs appear to date back as far as 10,500 years ago, and possibly even 14,800 years into our past. The vertical chain-like symbols are located in the Winnemucca Lake site, about 35 miles northeast of Reno, and consist of large, deeply carved grooves and dots that make complex designs on limestone boulders, and a number of small pits that may have been made with some type of hard rock scraper. The team published its findings in the June 2013 issue of the *Journal of Archeological Science.*

Landscape Art

Another form of rock art that occurs on a much bigger landscape is the Earth Figure, large designs, images, and symbols created in or on the actual ground itself. There are two kinds of Earth Figures:

Intaglios	Images that are created by removing rocks or landscape materials to reveal an image in the flat ground beneath.
Geoglyphs	Images created by placing or piling rocks or other materials on the surface of the ground to make a design or pattern.

Scientists believe that the world-famous Nazca Lines found in the Nazca Desert of southern Peru were created sometime between 400 AD and 700 AD. These geoglyphs depict hundreds of images, from simple lines and geometric shapes, to more sophisticated animal and bird shapes, as well as human figures. These geoglyphs, the largest of which measure more than 660 feet across, were made by removing reddish desert pebbles to reveal a shallow trench of the lighter, grayish-toned ground beneath, and are best visible from either the sky or nearby hilltops that surround the area.

Though most scholars agree on how the lines were created with possibly the use of simple stakes and tools and basic surveying techniques, the reason for the lines is still debated. The purpose of the lines has been alleged to be possible solstice and solar and lunar markers; tributes to the Sky Gods who could see the images from the heavens; a sort of crude planetarium that depicted the cosmology of the Nazca people; religious symbols depicting the worship of mountain and water deities; and other, more incredible ideas such as extraterrestrial air strips or an ancient airfield that was used by aliens the natives mistook for Gods.

Other such mysterious lines have been recently discovered in the Middle East, stretching from Syria to Saudi Arabia. Virtually unknown to the public, these geoglyphs, as described in the *LiveScience* article "Visible Only From Above, Mystifying Nazca Lines Discovered in Mideast" (September 2011) by Owen Jarus, are at least 2,000 years old and appear as wheels; stone structures in a variety of designs that have a common theme of a circle with spokes radiating inside. Many were created on lava fields and measure up to 230 feet across. The Jordan region alone contains more stone-built structures than the Nazca Lines, covering a far more extensive area, according to David Kennedy, professor of classics and ancient history at University of Western Australia.

This new discovery was part of a long-term aerial reconnaissance project examining archeological sites across Jordan. Though Kennedy and his colleagues have found not only wheel-shaped stone structures, but stone landscapes including kites, used for funneling and killing animals; pendants, used in burial rites; and walls that go on for hundreds of feet but seem to have no purpose, they still have no clue what these structures meant to the builders thousands of years ago. The spokes within the wheel structures have not been found to align with any planetary or cosmic phenomena and don't seem to have any larger sense or pattern, and might simply have served as places of reverence, ritual, and worship, as did other stone circles such as henge monuments in Great Britain (discussed in Chapter 7).

Other Art Forms

Visual arts of indigenous cultures took other forms throughout history, often related to the environment and materials found naturally nearby. Carvings have been found on deer bones in South Korean caves dating back 40,000 years, and artifacts dating back even as far as 100,000 years, during the Middle Paleolithic era, show signs of being expressive art rather than just useful tools. During the Lithic period, also defined as the Paleo-Indian period in North America from 18,000 BC to 8000 BC cave and rock paintings were not the only means of expression for those who wished to leave their mark via a visual medium. Bone carvings and beadwork, basketry, pottery and ceramics, crude jewelry and sculpture, even totem poles and woodcarvings allowed for a more multi-dimensional form of communication.

Earliest bone carvings in America date back more than 10,000 years in the Vero Beach area of Florida, where the bones of humans were found along with those of extinct animals of the Pleistocene period. The bones were of mammoths or mastodons and featured etchings of anatomically correct mammoths. Bones and even skulls were used for painting as well, progressing into the more sophisticated use of baskets, stone tools and arrowheads, banner stones, wood, and ceramic pottery of the Archaic period, from 8000 BC to 800 BC. Mask carvings and the use of walrus and sperm whale ivory appeared in the Alaskan and Canadian arctic and Greenlandic Inuit cultures more than a thousand years ago; they were used for both ritualistic and decorative means. Every culture has its progressive history of visual expression, and soon even items such as tools, baskets, pots, and clothing items were proving to be modes of such expression even as they were useful and functional. Masks and beadwork often held supernatural or shamanistic symbolism and were widely used in hunting and other rituals, sometimes to honor a deity and sometimes to ward off an evil one.

Totem poles are an intriguing form of art native to the Pacific Northwest indigenous cultures, carved from the trunks of nearby red cedar trees. The word *totem* is from the Ojibwe *odoodem,* which means "kinship group" and totem poles were symbols of a family clan, usually one of wealth and privilege, almost like a wooden coat of arms or family crest.

Totem carving may have originated in the islands of Haida Gwaii, where pole carving soon spread to neighboring islands before reaching the coastal tribes living along British Columbia into Northern Washington State. Because the poles were carved intricately, they suggested the use of more sophisticated iron and steel tools, which eventually led to even more complex carved items.

Often, a totem would describe a complete lineage, or a family history in visual images, but many are mainly done for artistic means. There are poles that even incorporate specific historical events and cultural beliefs that may only be identifiable to the family clan that "owns" the pole, and poles that have the specific goal of shaming a clan or family, as in a giant scarlet letter. Today, we would put a big sign on someone's front yard, but before writing developed, people were celebrated, and humiliated, with art objects.

House-front totem poles were objects that described the success of the family for all to see, and totems appeared to be less objects of worship (if ever at all) and more of a way to brag to the locals of your clans achievements and lineage, done in a vertical order of importance, which may have led to the popular saying "low man on the totem pole." Nowadays, we have McMansions and expensive cars parked in the driveway to display our status, but the totem pole served to let the natives know who was top dog in the hood.

Ochre—Primitive Paint

Primitive artists had dirt, rock, bone, caves, trees, and other natural canvases upon which to paint and carve and draw and etch. Ancient artists had the pleasure of using more developed means, such as papyrus and cloth. Some of the earliest painted rock and cave art was done with ochre, a natural iron oxide used as a pigment, which leaves a reddish or yellowish or brownish stain that was even used on pottery and human tattoo work. Ochre was said to ward off insects and mosquitoes as well, and was often mixed with crushed bone, charcoal, and shells to give it more texture. Ochre was used in the some of the earliest known cave art sites at Blombos, South Africa, where pieces of ochre incised with an abstract design have been dated as far back as 70,000 years ago. Scientists have found earlier signs of ochre use at Blombos and other sites as old as 165,000 years.

Scooped abalone shells and other such objects have been discovered that indicate that ochre was stirred and mixed like we do with modern paint to find the right color before painting. According to *Science Now*'s report titled "Prehistoric Painters Planned Ahead" (October 13, 2011), Christopher Henshilwood of the University of Bergen in Norway and his colleagues discovered two ochre-processing "toolkits" at Blombos that date back 100,000 years ago with "a technique called optically stimulated luminescence, which measures how long grains of sand in archaeological layers have been hidden from sunlight. The toolkits, found only 16 centimeters apart in the same layer, were very similar: Both consisted of abalone shells filled with a mixture of ochre, crushed bone, and charcoal." The group told *Science Now*: "Inside both shells were chunks of ochre-stained quartzite rock apparently used to grind the mixture. One of the shells also had part of the forearm bone of a canid, possibly a wolf or fox, which the team thinks might have been used to stir the paint or transfer it out of the shell."

Dating Art From the Past

Dating prehistoric and even ancient art is difficult, but in general we can answer a few questions about the age of art created by humans.

The earliest art came during the Stone Age, between 300,000 and 700,000 years ago. The Stone Age was divided into three main eras:

Paleolithic (2,500,000 BC–10,000 BC)	Hunter-gatherers
Mesolithic (10,000 BC–4000 BC)	Beginnings of fishing and farming
Neolithic (4000 BC–2000 BC)	Farming

The earliest art was petroglyph and rock art, which then led to engraving, sculpture in bone, wood, and stone, cave painting, relief sculpture, and ceramic pottery, followed by architecture. The first artists lived during the Lower Paleolithic Era, approximately 1,000,000 BC–300,000 BC and were descendants of Homo erectus. When language and art began to appear in the European region during the Upper Paleolithic, between 40,000 BC and 10,000 BC, scholars believe primitive art took on an aesthetic quality as opposed to strictly a functional one.

Figurines and sculptures were other early forms of artistic expression, as was ceramic art and pottery, which was often as decorative as it was useful. Carvings and images of humans were popular motifs, along with animals, rituals, and nature, much of which conveyed a distinct emphasis on fecundity, especially with the female form. Many of the earliest known sculptures of female figures are the European "Venus" figurines, which exaggerated female breasts and genitalia, belly and hips and thighs, and were meant to portray a fertile woman. Other such imagery was clear Goddess worship, but always the images focused on the reproductive and seductive qualities of the female body.

One of the oldest Stone Age figurines is the Venus of Berekhet Ram, thought to date from 500,00 BC to 230,000 BC. This figurine, although crudely formed and almost hard to distinguish, was discovered by archeologist N. Goren-Inbar during an excavation on the Golan Heights between Syria and Israel in 1981. The figurine shows groove-like incisions that were made by some sharp-edged stone and appear to be a female body. A sister figurine, called the Venus of Tan-Tan, was discovered in Morocco and is said to be so similar it could have been carved by the same person.

Later Venus figurines became much more sophisticated and detailed, and during the Bronze Age, obviously the use of bronze overtook the crude nature of working with rock and stone. The Bronze Age (3000 BC–1200 BC) was the age of metallurgy and the use of bronze, gold, and silver metalwork, and ceramics prevailed.

❦

Piercing the Past of Pottery

China not only gave the world the first use of porcelain, but may have been the first to introduce pottery as well. Bits of ceramic pottery have been discovered in the Xianrendong Cave in Jiangxi, China, dating back 20,000 years. Many scholars had believed that the first pottery originated in Japan, but this new discovery suggests that it may have started in China and spread quickly to Japan, where pottery around the same age has been discovered, rather than the other way around.

Pottery and earthenware are made with various forms of clay, and can either be considered "greenware," which means they are not fired to solid form in a kiln and remain rather soft and shapeable, or "fired," which uses the heat of a kiln to set the clay. Pottery is mainly functional, but has a history of being equally decorative, utilizing a number of incisions on the surface or underglaze decorations, as well as in-glaze or on-glaze decorations of more modern times.

Ancient kilns used for firing might have used a mound, a trench pit, or a bonfire pit before the progression to brick or stone kilns that burned wood or coal. In order for a culture to use pottery, it must first have access to usable clay; large deposits existed in China, where pottery may have originated. Earliest forms of pottery were shaped by hand using a process called "pinch and coil" to produce the vessel-like effect. The first potter's wheel appeared in Mesopotamia between 6000 BC and 4000 BC. Porcelain first appeared on the scene during the Tang Dynasty in China (618–906 CE). Pottery use would spread and become prevalent in Japan, India, Europe, and the Islamic world, and was independently developed in Sub-Saharan Africa as far back as 11,000 BC and South America around the same time, as more and more ways of finding, processing, and firing clay became available. Each culture had a style of its own, often reflecting the character of the culture itself, while other pottery appeared to be purely decorative. Who wants to look at a boring pot?

By the way, pieces of pottery are called "sherds." Remember that the next time you drop a ceramic flowerpot on the kitchen floor!

Later Art Forms

The art of the later Iron Age (1500 BC–200 BC) introduced the great era of Classical Antiquity and the flourishing of Greek sculpture and pottery, Roman art, Indian art, and early Chinese pottery. With the spread of ancient civilizations throughout the Mesopotamian region between 3,500 BC and 331 BC, the Sumerians began to build temples, ziggurats, and sculptures of the gods, while the Akkadians, Babylonians, Assyrians, and Persians developed more sophisticated forms of artistic and architectural expression, including the stele, used to engrave the first uniform code of laws in 2,000 BC (the written Code of Hammurabi of the Babylonian Empire).

Egyptian art began to flourish between 3200 BC and 1340 BC with tombs, pyramids, and afterlife. Egyptian art and sculpture centers on powerful authority figures, Gods and Goddesses. and dynastic art, as well as painted relief sculptures. Egyptians created the first seated and freestanding statues around 2,800 BC and designed elaborate megalithic tombs and massive temples, as well as sculptures made of gold leaf, copper, and lapis lazuli.

The ancient art of the advanced cultures of China, India, Egypt, Greece, Rome, and other regions was the final progression toward a form or system of writing (which the next chapter will cover). Much of this art was religious in nature, as the art of Ancient Egypt, because, quite simply, the cultures had developed a large focus on their own religious beliefs and growing traditions. Egyptian art, which was proportional and orderly, and featured clean lines and simple shapes, depicted the deities and the Pharaohs, whom many considered divine and were presented as God-Kings, of their time. Power and order was highly symbolized, as were the symbols of each God or Goddess, and the colors associated with them and the region itself. Yellow obviously was used to represent the sun god, and red represented power, vitality, and even control in war. Animals were featured just as often as humans and deities.

The great monumental tombs and edifices like the Sphinx and the Pyramids were art and architecture in action, and tombs, mastabas, and pyramids of the Old Kingdom led to the more sophisticated sculptures of the Middle Kingdom and then to the royal tombs and temple complexes of the New Kingdom period, which was the time of Tutankhamen and Ramses II and the funerary text, the Book of the Dead.

According to the Oriental Institute of the University of Chicago, art was used in ancient Egypt as a form of communication for those who could not yet read. It was also used to document daily life for future generations, as well as to decorate and create objects for funerary and religious rituals. Art wasn't just to look at. It meant something, including the wall murals common in ancient Egyptian buildings no doubt created by teams of artists with a common purpose and message. Because of Egypt's importance for almost 30 centuries as the preeminent civilization of the Western world, there is a huge field of study called Egyptology that focuses on the art, architecture, and archeology of this hugely influential cultural powerhouse.

Greek Influence

Greek art of the Iron Age began in Europe around 1500 BC around the same time China was creating their first bronze sculptures. Egyptian, Greek, and Etruscan art would then influence Roman art. Greek art was divided into three distinct eras:

> 1. The Archaic (600 BC–500 BC).
>
> 2. The Classical (500 BC–323 BC).
>
> 3. The Hellenistic (323 BC–27 BC).

The evolution of Greek art corresponded with their emphasis on humanistic education, much of which is mirrored in their sculptures, ceramics, and architecture, which glorifies the human being. The Etruscans lived in Italy during the sixth and fifth centuries BC and introduced more stylized Bronze sculpture as well as tombs and sarcophagi. Romans would, of course, attempt to wipe out both Greek and Etruscan art and culture, but fail, before going on to create their own signature style that introduced more monumental architecture, giant fresco paintings, and sculpture and figures of the Gods and Goddesses they pilfered from the Greek and Etruscan cultures and renamed in Roman language.

Greek art went through four distinct periods:

1. The Geometric Period (also known as the Mycenaean Period of between 1600 BC and 800 BC)—Imagery often used on pottery, ceramic vessels, cups, and grave markers featured geometric angular patterns and sometimes stick people engaged in battle.

2. The Archaic Period (700 BC–500 BC)—There was a flourish of narrative iconography on vases and sculptures, in paintings, and bronze sculptures that have since been melted down and recycled.

3. The Classical Period (500 BC–323 BC)—The high point or golden age of ancient Greece. Vase painting grew more sophisticated, and bronze statues and sculptures flourished. Major architecture of this period were temples dedicated to Gods and Goddesses of Greek mythology, such as the Parthenon of Athens, a temple dedicated to the Goddess Athena.

4. The Hellenistic Period (323 BC–146 BC)—Preceded the incorporation of the Greek empire within the Roman Empire, and this period ended when Greece actually became a part of the Roman Empire. During this period, Greek art and culture spread, and influenced many regions throughout the world. Art and sculpture became more action-oriented, often depicting violence and warlike, and again featured a variety of mythological deities and creatures.

Hellenistic Greek art highly influenced Romans, who had by then taken over all things Greek, and became obvious in the Roman copies of actual Greek works. One of Rome's greatest artistic offerings was found in or near the famed city of Pompeii, buried under the ashes of the eruption of Mt. Vesuvius in 79 AD. Painted walls with scenes taken from Roman mythology were found alongside mosaics, minute pieces of colored stones that made up pictorial scenes, something the Roman artists were noted for. Again, mythology was a major theme in Roman art, sculpture, statuary, architecture, and pottery. (In the next chapter, we'll find out why.)

This crash course in art history is necessary because each era could take up 10 books of its own. The idea, though, is an obvious progression of sophisticated means of artistic expression, using the means each culture had, along with new discoveries and developments, to tell others about the human experience. Whether we are talking ancient Japanese ceramic pottery, or a spout vessel from Peru that is shaped like a crab, or a figurine of a Goddess, or a tomb shaped like a Sphinx, the art of primitive and ancient times was meant to tell us something, to convey information about the particular environment, culture, or historical times the creators lived in. From the ancient tomb murals of Korea and the kiln-fired pottery of ancient Japan, to the megalithic engravings and elaborate drawings on Neolithic pottery in central Europe, or the first-century-BC engraved mirrors with music motifs found in Celtic regions, and the ceremonial bronze axes and ornamental helmets of western and central Europe, and the expressive and distinctive gold Moche headdresses of Peru, art has been a visual means of saying something, of telling our place in the world and our status in our own homes, neighborhoods, and villages, as well as how we, throughout the course of history, have seen the world around us—how we've understood it and then tried to pass on that understanding to others.

The progression of art from primitive and prehistoric to the more classical, ancient historical eras showed a distinct change in the focus of those creating the art. Where before, rock and cave art and other older forms emphasized animals, nature, hunting, and survival, later art focused on the cosmos, reproduction, war, battles, territorialism, Gods and Goddesses, religious beliefs and rituals, and the mysteries of death and the afterlife. The human body was examined, carved, engraved, painted, and sculpted, and the association of women and sexual reproduction was given special status along with important deities and mythical creatures that represented the powers of nature we did not yet have the scientific means to understand.

3-D Art

The proliferation of three-dimensional art, with sculpture, pottery, masks, and figurines, allowed even greater expression than just flat rock and wall art. As tools grew more sophisticated, so did our ability to create with them.

And each culture has its own artistic and archeological history, even as all cultures are intertwined by the spread of information and ideas.

Information exchange theory is an actual study and modeling of information exchange processes among interacting agents. In a fascinating paper titled "Art As Information: Explaining Upper Paleolithic Art in Western Europe," authors C. Michael Barton, G.A. Clark, and Allison E. Cohen examined the temporal and spatial distribution of art during the Upper Paleolithic era and looked at how this art and, even more specifically, style performed an important social function at the time—that of information exchange. Their research was concluded to be indicative and applicable to other regions as well. To the researchers, style was a marker for how art was used to inform. Information exchange theory posits that stylistic elements are primarily used to convey information if they serve no functional or utilitarian purpose. They use the example of an artistic object of a spear thrower that is functional and has a purpose that can affect individual or group fitness. But if that spear thrower is carved in the likeness of a horse, it is stylistic and therefore selectively neutral by definition. The horse likeness is meant to convey specific information, maybe of a specific clan or tribe or group of people to whom that horse is meaningful; the image of the spear thrower itself is functional in nature. Art and the adaptation of art to the size of alliance networks also serve as a channel to spread the flow of information. The bigger the alliance networks, the more means of information exchange there is. The authors wrote: "Information will tend to flow along the channels defined and maintained through the negotiation of alliances. Alliances are of variable commitment and duration, are defined in many ways and at many scales, have many functions, some of which have material correlates." Information along channels of alliances could be used to increase the environmental knowledge and reach for resources.

One way art and style serve to spread the flow of information is through the distinct style, which is indicative of the culture, social beliefs, location, experiences, and interpretations of those experiences of the community in which that style originates. Style is a language, in a sense, that can communicate information via the visible manifestation of art.

Visual means of saying something, of spreading information—even hiding and embedding information—preceded the more complex written style of communication. Just as a child will first draw crude images with big fat crayons before he or she has the dexterity and intelligence to pick up a pencil, or in this day and age, a tablet or computer, and type out a novel, art paved the way for greater methods, modes, and means of transmitting knowledge and information. Although a picture certainly is worth a thousand words, it appears that progress and evolution demanded a way for us to express information in ten thousand, a hundred thousand, even a million words.

Thus, we began to write.

Of Gods and Goddesses: The Rise of the Written Word

Myths are public dreams, dreams are private myths.
—Joseph Campbell

Thus we hope to teach mythology not as a study, but as a relaxation from study; to give our work the charm of a story-book, yet by means of it to impart a knowledge of an important branch of education.
—Thomas Bulfinch

Science must begin with myths, and with the criticism of myths.

—Karl Popper

The problem with oral tradition is that often in the verbal passing on of information, things get misinterpreted, misconstrued, and mis-communicated. We've all experienced this whenever we've passed on a message from someone else and forgot to include a few key words, or got a piece of gossip that was embellished by several people before we heard it, or those family stories that always seem to be told a little differently by each successive generation.

The problem with symbols and art is that they cannot always be properly interpreted unless we were the ones who actually drew them.

Never can we really know what was intended to be communicated by a symbol, a drawing, a petroglyph, or even an elaborate painting. Heck, we still can't even seem to figure out exactly what put that smirk on the Mona Lisa's face!

Thus, the need for a more sophisticated, adaptive, and complex means for passing on information arose both progressively and spontaneously in the form of the written word. Once our ancestors developed a writing system with letters or numbers or even hieroglyphs, they gained the ability to communicate in more detail and hopefully convey more information about who they were, how they lived, and even what they believed.

Rare is the person who writes before he or she draws. Rare is the person who writes even before he or she speaks those first garbled words in baby talk. There is an order to expression that evolves as we do.

In the Beginning...

The Sumerians of ancient Mesopotamia are often credited with the creation of the earliest form of writing, dating back to approximately 3500 BC. This writing was really nothing more than pictograms on clay tablets, intended to convey an object or idea, and was not true writing systems as we think of them. But the people of the Mesopotamian region are credited with the invention of "cuneiform," a precursor to writing systems of a more alphabetized nature that evolved from basic lines and scratches in clay to more detailed "wedge-shaped signs" that were embedded into the clay with a reed stylus or other pointed object. Cuneiform functioned both phonetically, representing a sound, as well as semantically, representing a meaning, and took communication to a whole new level beyond just pictures of objects. Cuneiform became standardized so that it would be recognizable to larger groups of people, and was used for more than 3,000 years to communicate information in Sumerian, Babylonian, Akkadian, Hittite, and Old Persian, among others.

Around the same time, 3100 BC, the Sumerians invented numerals, which allowed them to document measurement and amount of an object in question, and advanced their communications from the simplicity of pictographs to a more ideographic system, where a symbol represents an idea or concept.

The first "true city" is thought to be Uruk, in Sumer, in the southern Mesopotamian region that today is known as Iraq. This is the cradle of civilization, where a progression away from more survival-based existence into a more cultural focus was obvious, and the need arose for people to keep track of things, especially items that were traded, sold, and bartered. Writing, therefore, was an adaptive necessity that also allowed for local laws, customs, rules, and rituals to be recorded in a more durable form than oral communication permitted, and provided a true record-keeping method for commercial transactions by temple officials who were given the role of keeping track of the movement of grain, animals, and other items sold from their stores and farms. One of the leading markers of a true civilization, according to archeologist V. Gordon Childe, author of *Man Makes Himself,* is the creation of standards of measurement and writing.

According to the Oriental Institute of the University of Chicago, the invention of writing was the dawn of the information revolution. Writing was a great cultural and technological advancement that allowed information in the form of news and ideas and innovations to be carried over much greater distances, without having to rely on the memory of the messenger. Egypt developed a writing system shortly after Sumer, about 3000 BC (although some archeologists suggest an Egyptian origin about 3400 BC), that, like cuneiform, may have been for record-keeping purposes, as well as for monumental displays of deities. Hieroglyphs are the most widely recognized script, even though the last hieroglyphic inscription dates all the way back to 394 AD. The word itself comes from the Greek *hieros,* for "sacred," and *gluptien,* for "carved in stone," but ancient Egyptians also developed other systems through time.

From 2300 BC to 700 BC, the hieratic script was developed. This handwritten script was used for administrative and non-monumental texts up until the introduction of the "demotic" script of the Late Period of 661 BC–332 BC. Demotic script was a more abbreviated version of the hieratic, and then led to Coptic script in the first century AD.

China had meanwhile developed its own writing about 1200 BC as a means of telling the future, using hot rods to create patterns in "oracle bones" made of cracked oxen shoulder blades and turtle shells. Chinese scripts also evolved and developed with the times, and for different purposes, with clerical script appearing about 200 BC for keeping records, and calligraphy, considered the highest art form, featuring characters that are drawn in perfect proportion, balance, and order. Scholars believe Chinese writing developed independently of the Sumerian/Egyptian system because it bore little resemblance to the cuneiform and instead had the characteristics of a logographic system, using symbols to represent whole words.

Later systems arose in the Indus region of northwestern India and what is now Pakistan about 3000 BC that suggested they were more of a proto-writing system, or, a system of symbols, rather than the logographic system of use in China. Mexico and other Meso-American cultures adopted their own independent writing systems later, about 600 BC.

From Proto-Writing to True Writing

Writing evolved through many stages to develop from proto-writing of simple and obvious images and symbol systems, and the true writing of an alphabetic system. Those stages, in the correct order of development, according to *A Study of Writing*, by Dr. Ignace J. Gelb, professor of linguistics at the University of Chicago, are:

1. Ideographic—Basically composed of pictures and easily discernable images, with no relationship between the written or inscribed symbol and any speech sound.

2. Logographic—A written sign stands for an actual word in spoken language.

3. Syllabic—A symbol or glyph represents a single syllable, a consonant followed by a vowel, and sometimes ending with another consonant.

4. Alphabetic—A symbol or glyph represents an actual sound, where there is a single character for every single sound.

Proto-writing to true writing also follows a basic three-stage series of developmental milestones that begin with *picture writing systems,* using glyphs that directly represent an object or idea; the *transitional system,* where glyphs refer not just to an object or idea but to that object's actual name; and the *phonetic system,* where glyphs refer to sounds of either a whole word (logogram), a syllable, or an elementary alphabetic sound.

A True Alphabet

The first true alphabet may have come about the late eighth century BC from the Greeks, who were the first to attribute sounds to both vowels and consonants, but they borrowed heavily from an earlier system courtesy of the Phoenicians. The letters and orders of letters of both systems are the same, but for the inclusion of separate letters for vowels in the Greek. From the Greek alphabet, the modern alphabets of Europe evolved.

However, there is a second theory as to the origins of the alphabet that places its birth in Ancient Egypt about 1800 BC, courtesy of Semitic workers that lived along the eastern coast of the Mediterranean. This was a short, 22-character alphabet with names and a fix order for the characters, and was spread through the region most likely by Phoenician traders. Once the Greeks got hold of it, they introduced vowels into the existing alphabet to create their own. In fact, the first two words of the Greek system are *alpha* and *beta,* which put together made the name *alphabet.*

Just as with visual communicative systems, writing systems soon spread or were independently developed as each culture felt the distinct need to create one, with the progress of trade, economic development, and necessity of recording more complex religious, administrative, and legal documentation. Writing may have begun as a means of expressing laws and rules and numbers and who bought how many sheep from whom for how much and when; it soon evolved into a form of artistic expression as well. Information didn't always have to be basic, survival-based, and mundane. The evolution of writing did not happen quickly, or overnight, because of the factors of each culture involved. The symbols and glyphs that once conveyed all a culture needed to know or pass on became more complex and more evolved, and the need for a more sophisticated system arose, as the cultures themselves grew more complex and evolved. Again we are reminded of the child who graduates from crayons and blank paper to pens and pencils and lined paper to pads and computers—from scrawling his or her name on a drawing of the sun and a flower to writing complex, informative books.

The story of expression is, indeed, the story of our own evolution.

Sometimes information told its own stories, in its own way. For ancient civilizations, myth and religious writings became the premier mode of expressing ideas that informed others of the fundamental beliefs of a culture. Because scientific understanding may have been in short supply, this was often accomplished by ascribing the workings of nature to Gods, Goddesses, and other entities. Think about it. Today, we know what causes thunder and lightning. We have the scientific acumen and knowledge to grasp that, and it isn't mysterious, even though we stand in awe of the workings of the natural world. But to our ancient ancestors, it appeared to be a much different world. Nature was filled with her own stories to be told—and understood.

The First Stories

The first stories told were no doubt myths and creation/origin tales that gave some structure to ideas and concepts about the origin of a culture—who they thought they were, how they got here, and their specific place in the bigger picture. What is a myth?

According to Dictionary.com, a myth is:

1. A traditional or legendary story, usually concerning some being or hero or event, with or without a determinable basis of fact or a natural explanation, especially one that is concerned with deities or demigods and explains some practice, rite, or phenomenon of nature.

2. Stories or matter of this kind: *realm of myth.*

3. Any invented story, idea, or concept: *His account of the event is pure myth.*

4. An imaginary or fictitious thing or person.

5. An unproved or false collective belief that is used to justify a social institution.

The word comes to us from the Latin and Greek *mythos,* which means "story, word," and originates from about 1820 AD.

Myths we are most familiar with act as both a fictional and, as we will see, potentially truthful account of history and creation according to a particular region or culture. Myths serve to explain the world around us, with common themes, motifs, and symbols that can be found across the globe. People often confuse myths with fables, legends, and folklore, which may have some mythical elements, but real myths appear to be less about entertainment and more about passing on important religious, spiritual, or natural information in the form of fantastical stories involving deities and creatures that most likely did not exist, or did exist albeit in a much less fantastical form than the myth describes.

Carried on via both oral and written traditions, the academic description of a myth is a story that a particular culture holds true, though it may not be true for others, but myth can also serve as a metaphor for what is beyond the direct understanding or consciousness. Joseph Campbell, no doubt the world's most well-known and highly respected comparative mythologist, called myth "a metaphor transparent to transcendence," meaning beyond our direct and ordinary state of comprehension and consciousness. In *The Power of Myth*, Campbell writes:

> Mythology is not a lie, mythology is poetry, it is metaphorical.
> It has been well said that mythology is the penultimate truth—
> penultimate because the ultimate cannot be put into words. It
> is beyond words. Beyond images, beyond that bounding rim of
> the Buddhist Wheel of Becoming. Mythology pitches the mind
> beyond that rim, to what can be known but not told.

Myths are not absolute truth, but can be described as relative truth to the culture that believes in the myth, in that the myth itself tells of the perception of that culture and of how it brings order to the chaos around it. Myths are the stories we've told as a species that are embedded with truths, realities, and even historical events such as earthquakes, wars, and meteor strikes. But they are not pure news reporting.

Professor of history of religions and author Mircea Eliade looks at myth as a foundational element of religion and essential to it. Other religious scholars believe that myths are an inherent part of religion, because they are simply sacred texts that contain embedded in them wisdom and truths that may be divinely inspired.

If we look at the traditional religious texts and their stories, we might say we are looking at myths that express profound truths to the cultures that believe in that particular religious tradition. Not all religious stories may qualify as myth, but some seem obvious in their comparisons. The stories of the Bible can be said to be the mythology of the Middle East, filled with parables and legends and lore of deities and humans with superpowers and miraculous events and great floods and wars—men born of virgins and angels and demons, all the same fodder for other myths from other regions but with perhaps just different names. Myths and religious stories share many similarities, which include:

- Creation stories of voids, nothingness, and paradise before the beginning of time.
- Stories of deities that undergo death and resurrection; the life-death-rebirth motif.
- An *axis mundi* or cosmic or world center.
- Themes of good versus evil and karmic retribution.
- A hero or chosen deity who undertakes a challenge or journey.
- A great flood.

There are categories of myths as well, which include:

- Myth as origin and creation story.
- Myth as dreams and visions.
- Myths of archetypes.
- Myths of sacred histories.
- Myth as proto-scientific knowledge.
- Myth as religious, spiritual, or metaphysical truth.
- Myth as personal challenge/hero's journey.
- Myths of power hierarchies.
- Myth as moral, ethical, and principal beliefs.

Though others are quick to dismiss both myth and religious stories of creation, life, death, and rebirth as pure fiction, that may not be the case at all. Information in the form of historical, cultural, and even scientific truth could be encoded within the tales of heroism, redemption, and renewal, of life and love and survival. Hiding in the tales of Gods and Goddesses, of creatures and beasts and wars and battles, of talking trees and burning bushes and shape-shifting humans and animals we might actually learn what the ancients knew about the world around them, and how it worked.

Common Themes, Motifs, and Symbols

For both myth and religion, certain themes, motifs, and symbols appear throughout and across cultural and social borders. These similarities speak of a common understanding of often complex and "supernatural" elements of existence, such as creation and our place in the cosmic scheme of things. Creation stories and myths from the world over talk of order and form arising out of chaos or a dark void of nothingness, of light and wound as creative sources, of an unimagined and shapeless Universe that is given form via the will and intention of a deity or deities, of an order of Gods and lesser Gods and then humans emerging from the primordial soup, of a division of the cosmic all into a number of realms, most notably the three of earth, sky, and water—or heaven, hell, and earth.

Some of the common themes, motifs, and symbols are:

1. Fate and destiny.
2. Retribution and revenge.
3. Love and marriage/procreation/beauty.
4. Cycle of birth/death/rebirth/natural cycles/creation/ destruction.
5. Dangers of greed/lust/arrogance.
6. Redemption.

7. The hero's journey/quest.

8. Superpowers.

9. Acquiring power/wisdom/life lessons.

10. Control of self/others/Nature.

11. Youth vs. elderly.

12. Searching for God/the search for the missing God.

These are but a few of the kinds of myths and even religious stories that have been passed down throughout history. They mirror the common experiences and challenges of humanity and the quest to understand both the personal/individual and collective roles we play. It doesn't matter where the myth comes from, because these commonalities prevail. Names of deities and other characteristics will be changed, but ultimately we get the same stories, told over and over again. In the case of religious myths, the theme of enlightenment is much more prevalent than in traditional myths, where the hero's journey, clashes between deities, and love often take center stage.

The Great Flood Myth

One of the most common themes in myth is that of a great flood that was sent by a God or Gods to punish and destroy sinful earth dwellers. The Great Flood myth also parallels the many global creation myths involving life emerging from the primeval waters or Primordial Ocean. Some of the greatest epics ever told are flood stories, such as the Mesopotamian "Epic of Gilgamesh," written on 12 large tablets from about 650 BC that tell a story that may date back to earlier than 2000 BC in which a man named Utnapishtim is told by the God, Ea, to build a huge vessel to protect his family, friends, and even animals from a pending flood, a lot like a man named Noah in the Judeo-Christian Bible. The Hindu have the Satapatha Brahmana and the tale of first man, Manu, being warned of a pending flood and told to build a boat.

The Sumerian flood myth was the Ziusudra epic, and the Chinese have their Gun-You myth of a father-son team that attempt to control the flood waters, as well as the oral tradition of the Hei Miao myth in which Thunder is angry and decides to drown the earth, with only two survivors left to carry on humanity. Interestingly, the Chinese flood myths deviate from the normal flood myth theme of punishment by God/Gods. In the Chinese myths, the flooding is usually the cause of natural disaster or some mysterious element.

The Greek have their Deucalion, who because of his prudence and piety is allowed to load up an ark with his wives, kids, and animals when God unleashes a flood on the earth. In the Roman flood myth, Jupiter wants to destroy humanity by fire but not wanting to get burned himself, decides on a flood instead. The Welsh myth involves the Lake of Llion bursting and flooding the lands, with Dwyan and Dwyfach escaping in a big ship along with pairs of every living creature. The Southwest Tanzania myth also has God telling two men to take seeds and animals onto a ship with them as floodwaters rise. In this myth, they even send out a dove to see if it locates dry land. Sound familiar?

The flood of Noah and the flood of Gilgamesh have many commonalities:

Both were global floods sent by a God/Gods to punish man's wickedness or sinfulness.
Both have a righteous hero who is told to build a boat.
Both were told to take family and animals of all species.
Both used the release of birds to seek dry land.
Both boats landed on a mountain.
Both men were blessed after the flood.

There is much argument over which came first—the Gilgamesh epic or the Hebrew account of the Great Flood—but regardless, this kind of shared mythology is common, and these are but a few of the many flood tales, many of which contain the same elements over and over again, most notably a boat or ark, pairs of animals on board, and a pure man or hero surviving to start the human race anew. Though scientists argue over the actual date these floods might have occurred, and no doubt there is a suggestion that each region may have its own origins for its own flood myths (including overflowing rivers, global, or regional climate change, torrential rains, tsunamis...), there are also those who suggest that perhaps there never was a real flood at all, and that the theme is a sort of archetype or symbol of a transformative cleansing of a flawed race into a purer state, or the punishment and redemption of the sinful at the hands of angry Gods, and their opportunity to "get things right" somewhere fresh and new.

Maybe we all have our own personal flood myth.

Codes and Morals

The Greek and Romans were noted for incorporating their ethical codes and morals into their myths, which often indicated the behaviors that were desired and rewarded in society, and those that would be punished. Most religious texts do the same thing, with parables and proverbs and moral stories of sin and forgiveness, meant to serve as moral guides for the culture of the time period. One difference between myth and religion is how the Gods were treated. Take the Judeo-Christian Bible, and you have a God that can do no wrong, is free of flaws, and is the ultimate moral authority. Yet in myth, Gods and Goddesses can be liars, cheaters, klutzes, dolts, and morons with their own flaws, even as they wield authority over the lesser beings. Mythological gods experience hubris and arrogance, anger and rage, violence and bloodlust;

and they steal women and animals that don't belong to them. But a religious God is usually represented as perfection that no mortal or even demigod can ever achieve.

Still, there are such amazing comparisons between both myth and religion, and pagan traditions and the religious traditions that came later, and we have to ask whether these common themes, motifs, and symbols were simply borrowed from one time and region by another, or experienced simultaneously or progressively as each culture developed. Maybe even a bit of both. We saw in Chapter 1 how information spreads, and often the motivations for spreading it vary. With myth and religious stories, that motivation is multi-pronged and could involve the evolution of belief, the spread of ritual and wisdom, the concurrent arising of consciousness and understanding, or, quite simply, one group of people ripping off the ideas, celebrations, and beliefs of another group of people, and as the case may have been, usurping those beliefs and incorporating them into the doctrine and dogma of the religion.

Though our job isn't to cause or create anger or controversy, we still owe it to readers to lay it on the table. And one of the most stunning examples of the progression of an idea or concept throughout the course of history, in terms of both myth and religious story, is the story of Jesus Christ, the messiah of the Christian world. Although no one knows the truth, there is plenty of intriguing circumstantial evidence to show that the Christ myth was in play long before Jesus was said to walk the earth—and may continue on until we have no more need of either myth or religion to encode the truth within story and fantasy. In our time, information is directly delivered, or so we like to believe.

The Jesus Model

Whether or not Jesus was a man, a myth, or a combination of the two is still up for debate among historians, scholars, and religious figures alike. Regardless, what we want to look at are the common elements between the life of Jesus Christ and many other characters from the past to show that myth evolves, develops, and changes in accordance with the needs of the people embracing that myth, but that core truths and foundational elements stay the same, no matter where the story ends up being told, and by whom. There are ideas that just don't change from culture to culture, because they convey powerful themes and even archetypal symbols that we all comprehend, no matter where we come from. Was Jesus an archetype?

Buddha was born of a virgin named Maya, called the Queen of Heaven. He also performed miracles and taught chastity, tolerance, and compassion. He was transfigured on a mount, and ascended to Nirvana, or heaven. He was called the Savior and Light of the World. He even fed 500 men from a basket of cakes and walked on water.

Horus, the son of Osiris and Isis in Egyptian myth, was born of the virgin Isis-Meri on December 25 in a cave. His birth was announced via a bright star in the east and attended by three kings. He was baptized, began teaching at age 30, had 12 disciples, raised a man from the dead, and walked on water. He was transfigured on a mount, betrayed then crucified, buried in a tomb, and then resurrected. He was often featured as a baby on Roman catacombs being held by his virgin mother, Isis.

The Sun God, Mithras, of Persia preceded the Christ story by more than 600 years and was the most popular pagan tradition at the time of Christianity. Mithras was born of a virgin on December 25, he had 12 companions, and performed miracles. He was identified with the lion and the lamb. He was buried in a tomb and arose three days later. His sacred day was Sun-Day. His resurrection occurred at what we now call Easter and was celebrated yearly on that date. Mithras is most associated with the Christ myth because of the prevalence of the Mithraic tradition at the dawn of Christianity, and the obvious common motifs presented in both myths. Sun God...Son of God.

Krishna, who many call the Indian messiah of Hinduism, was also born a virgin named Devaki, or Divine One. He is an incarnation of the Sun God, Vishnu, who rises on the winter solstice around December 21. His father was a carpenter, wise men and angels attended his birth, and he was given gifts of gold, frankincense, and myrrh. He raised the dead and healed lepers, the blind, and deaf, and worked miracles and wonders. He taught in parables, humbly washed the feet of others, cared for the poor and downtrodden, rose from the dead, and ascended to heaven. He is said to one day return to earth in a second coming to battle the Prince of Evil.

Even Dionysus, the Greek god of winemaking and the grape, and a fertility deity associated with often orgiastic rituals, could change water into wine, was born of a virgin on December 25, and was resurrected after death.

The story of Christ is filled with symbols and themes seen elsewhere in deities from Afghanistan (Bali) to Scandinavia (Odin/Thor) to Bermuda (Salivahana) to Greece (Kadmos) to the Aztecs (Quexalcote) to Esus of the Druids, often based upon much earlier pagan and earth-based belief systems. Some suggest that the 12 disciples of Christ and Mithras were the 12 signs of the zodiac depicted in human form. These myths may have even older roots in the "dying-and-rising god" (DARG) or "death-rebirth deity" of pagan cultures. The DARG idea suggests that a number of Gods of the ancient near east all had died and been resurrected in a formulaic manner that applied to each deity. These DARGs were almost cookie cutter, dating back to the third millennium BC, and were often associated with vegetation and nature deities that represented harvest and growing cycles.

Among these DARGS were Adonis, Tammuz and Osiris, Dionysus, Ra/Osiris/Orion, Baal, Eshmun, and perhaps even Jesus, who may have been a later version of the DARGs and more myth than literal. Female DARGS included Ishtar/Inanna, Bara, and Persephone, so this was not just a male motif, nor was it limited to the ancient near east, as the Japanese have their DARG in Izanami, the Norse Baldr, and the Aztec's Quetzalcoatl. This motif is popular in the field of comparative mythology, which looks for commonalities in the myths and religious beliefs of diverse cultures, and could either signify a God that went away physically and returned later, or literally died and was reborn in much the same way plants, flowers, trees, and crops "died" each winter season and were "reborn" in the spring. Ishtar and Persephone die every year and return, much in the same way as certain plant life. During their absence, there is no growth, but upon their return, the cycle of regrowth begins anew, thus the association of DARGs with many harvest rituals.

That the deities of both myth and religion should be so interchangeable shouldn't bring offense to anyone. Belief, if based at all on reality, would no doubt find common ground even as it spread from culture to culture throughout a period of time, with fundamental and often observable truths remaining encoded in the stories, rituals, and traditions as they evolved and grew.

⁂

One God, Many Names

Greek and Roman myths share many similarities, most notably their major deities. Many of the deities are the same, but with different names, showing a definite common influence from one region to another.

These are just a few of the deities that share characteristics and ruling domains. Because of regional proximity it makes sense that stories would infiltrate cultures and be adopted, and adapted, by and to specific cultures. Other global myths include similar deities; think of Odin and Thor of the Norse mythology as the counterparts of Zeus and Jupiter—the supreme ruler of Gods and the God of lightning/storms, signifying a collective understanding of nature and its cycles and the symbolic story-telling that was chosen to describe it.

Purpose	Greek	Roman
Supreme ruler of the Gods, lightning throwers	Zeus	Jupiter
God of the seas, carried a trident	Poseidon	Neptune
God of the Underworld and dead	Hades	Pluto
God of War	Ares	Mars
Goddess of agriculture	Athena	Minerva
Goddess of love and beauty	Aphrodite	Venus
Goddess of the hunt	Artemis	Diana
God of fire	Hephaestus	Vulcan
God of sleep	Hypnos	Somnus
Goddess of victory	Nike	Victoria
Goddess of grain	Demeter	Ceres
God of wine	Dionysus	Bacchus
God of the sky	Uranus	Uranus

What the heck were these stories all about, other than some guy named Thor playing with thunder and a hot babe named Venus who came out of the sea and made men melt, and a chick with snakes for hair and a bush that burned who gave out free wisdom to the chosen few, and winged horses that soar up to the top of mountains with Gods on their backs? Were they just fun and entertaining stories to pass the time—or were they meant to pass on much more than just an evening around the fire pit where oral traditions were soon to become the stories we read about in books made of pulp and ink?

E.O. James (1888–1972), an anthropologist in the field of comparative religion and former professor emeritus of the history and philosophy of religion in the University of London, writes in his book, *Creation and Cosmology: A Historical and Comparative Inquiry* that "[m]yth as it exists in a savage community, that is, in its living primitive form, is not merely a story told but a reality lived. It is not of the nature of fiction, such as we read to-day in a novel, but it is a living reality, believed to have once happened in primeval times, and continuing ever since to influence the world and human destinies." This attitude is mirrored by other experts in comparative religion and mythology, such as Joseph Campbell, author of *The Hero With a Thousand Faces* and *The Power of Myth,* and Mircea Eliade, author of *Images and Symbols* and *Cosmos and History: The Myth of the Eternal Return,* who see myth as more than just sheer story-telling for entertainment purposes. Myth had a purpose that went much deeper.

Comparative Mythology

Comparative mythology is a field of study devoted to examining myths from cultures and traditions all over the world to seek both differences and commonalities, and identify shared themes, characteristics, motifs, and even archetypes. Often looking at how myths evolve leads us to better understand how religious belief arises in a particular culture, and even gives a glimpse into political evolution as well. What people believe and the stories they tell themselves and pass on to future generations often describe more detail than we think about the lives they lead, even if these stories do also feature fantastical elements like deities and creatures that originate in the imagination.

The goal of comparative mythology is to find a "proto-mythology" that is the foundation from which all global myths may have been constructed. The same can be said for the fields of study of comparative religion and comparative cosmology—the attempt to find those common threads in the tapestry, or the first-laid cement framework before the walls went up. Myth, religion, and cosmology are all attempts to describe a culture's history, beliefs, and identity and place in the

Universal scheme of things. When scholars find common themes and motifs, it posits that ideas either spread from culture to culture, or developed simultaneously, and asks then how this happened.

It also begs the question: What is scientifically sound and what is pure fiction? How much of these myths and stories and religious beliefs were grounded in some true knowledge of the natural order of things, and how much were simply fantastical interpretations of how things worked? Two different schools of thought rule comparative mythology: Comparativists, who believe that a single myth was the origin point for all other myths that evolved around it, and Particularists, who suggest that different themes and elements in myth go against a common proto-myth, or as Joseph Campbell calls it, "monomyth."

Figure 3-1: A diagram of the path of the monomyth of the hero's journey.

The monomyth Campbell referred to was the hero's journey, which he describes at length in his seminal book, *The Hero With a Thousand Faces,* a theme found in most if not all narrative stories and myths, in which as he describes it, "A hero ventures forth from the world of common day into a region of supernatural wonder," where he then encounters all kinds of strange forces and entities, overcomes challenges, and emerges victorious, to then return a hero, often with newfound powers and abilities. The typical monomyth could be broken down into 17 stages within three main headings: the Departure/Call to Adventure; the Initiation/Trials and Temptations; and the Return/Mastery. If we think of the most widely known religious "stories" of the hero's journey we can see this pattern: Jesus Christ, Buddha, Moses, Osiris. Some of the more modern stories we know and love that follow this structure include *Star Wars,* where Luke Skywalker takes on the hero role, and the journeys of Frodo in the *Lord of the Rings* tales. Possibly the most famous monomyth example of all is the quest of King Arthur and the Arthurian Romances of chivalry, adventure, and the journey to knighthood and the discovery of the Holy Grail. Some people think the modern-day *Indiana Jones* movies also follow this monomyth. In fact, along with the three-act structure, the monomyth/hero's journey has become a very beloved and critical foundation for most of our favorite movies and television series, whether they are westerns, mysteries, or science fiction. Always, a lead character is being asked to mimic this mythical structure in a way that is satisfying to audiences on both a surface and subconscious level.

Many myths contain archetypes, or universal motifs, symbols, or symbolic patterns, ideas, and patterns of thought, and images that resonate with people on a global, collective level. Some of the most widely used archetypes include the dying God, as mentioned earlier, the Trickster, the scapegoat, the lost lover, the sexual wild woman, the damsel in distress, the rogue, the mentor/wise sage, the warrior, the great Mother, the powerful Father/Lord, and even elements within a story such as a Great Flood, the end of the world, virgin births, resurrection, and even sexual intercourse. The use of archetypes speaks to the subconscious, to the psyche, more so than to the conscious mind or intellect.

Three Popular Motifs

In myths from around the world, we are apt to find one of these three popular motifs present in one form or another. Each has its own archetypal symbolism, and all three represent the power and hold that the natural world had over our ancestors, who had yet to truly understand the way nature worked.

The Green Man

The Green Man motif is a symbol often found in carvings on churches, buildings, and homes that feature the face of a man surrounded by leaves or vegetation. Though the term was actually coined in 1939 in an article in *The Folklore Journal,* the Green Man, or Jack in the Green, was already a widely used motif and pagan fertility figure or nature spirit that represented the cyclical rebirth of nature each spring. Green Man motifs have appeared as far back as 400 AD.

Figure 3-2 : A Green Man sculpture on a Cistercian Abbey, Abbey Dore.

The World Tree/Axis Mundi

Present in many religious traditions and myths, from the Native American to the Meso-American to the Nordic and Siberian, a central "world tree" supports the heavens and connects the three levels of heaven, earth, and underworld together. In Norse myth, this tree is called Yggdrasil. In Hindu myth, it is the Ashvattha. To the Latvians, it was the Cosmic Tree. The Maya called it the *yax imix che.* Also associated with the concept of a "tree of life," the World Tree was often believed to connect different dimensions or realities, and today might be considered a wormhole! The World Tree was one of many *axis mundi* symbols, which represented the center of the world where the heaven connects with the earth. A natural object such as a vine or mountain, or a manmade object such as a tower, staircase, pole, or pillar, could also represent the axis mundi.

The Serpent/Snake

A serpent tempted Adam and Eve in the Garden of Eden. A naked-like being called Mucalinda protected Buddha from the elements after he achieved enlightenment. A dragon/serpent named Ouroboros swallows his own tail as a symbol of infinity, cycles, and eternity. The Nagar dragon eats from the roots of the Yggdrasil, the world tree of Norse myth. The Vision Serpent meant rebirth to the Mayan civilization. The two-headed serpent Nehebkau guarded the entrance to the underworld in Egyptian myth. The snake Goddess Wadjet, an Egyptian cobra, was even the first known oracle and is depicted as the crown of Egypt. Apollo killed the female serpent Python, who guarded the holy seat of Gaia at Delphi.

The serpent is one of mythology's oldest and most widely used symbols, and the snake is associated with the most ancient nature rites and rituals on record. The snake represents duality to some cultures, fertility to others, and was often the guardians of temples and sacred spaces. Because snakes shed their skin, they became associated with the cycles of birth, life, death, and rebirth, as well as healing, immortality, and transformation. Sea and cosmic serpents and many types of dragons are also common motifs and were sometimes given deity status, as with the Central American Quetzalcoatl or "feathered serpent," and the Ayida-Weddo of Haiti, a spirit of fertility and wife to the spirit father, Dan. Often, sacred serpents were depicted at or near World Trees, coiled around the trunk or under the tree itself. Another match-up of the Tree of Life and serpent symbolism is the caduceus of Hermes and the staff of Moses, both of which were rod-like sticks or staffs with coiled serpents entwined around them.

Myth and Psyche

Other than seeking that "monomyth," there is also the search for common psychological themes and elements (including Jungian arche-types), and historical and scientific accuracy, all of which might suggest parallels between cultures that may not have had the opportunity to actually communicate with one another. Mircea Eliade, who was a pro-fessor of the history of religions, even believed that myth was an essen-tial foundation of religion as well as a part of the human psyche. This was echoed by Joseph Campbell's own belief that myth allowed people a way to understand their own individual lives and was more than just some archaic attempt at story-telling.

That myths were "heroic legends" as once described by classicist Robert Graves, who authored a number of books on myth and religion, has never been argued. Clearly, myth and even religious parables, leg-ends, and stories tell us of the experiences and journeys of heroes and heroines and Gods and Goddesses, yet the common threads suggest that beneath those flashy tales of challenges overcome and obstacles met with are some real, factual details about life as they knew it. Legends and myths contained a seed of truth that may only be understandable if interpreted via the psyche, and not the mind and intellect. Myth and legend also document actual experiences as understood by those who experienced them, even if that language is primitive to us. Myth and legend serve to attempt to express a deeper spiritual connection we once had with our natural surroundings, thus giving deity-like powers to aspects of nature we didn't yet understand (like volcanoes, lightning, and earthquakes). Myth and legend also helped our ancestors articulate their idea of their place in the cosmos, again from their level of knowledge and understanding, not ours.

Joseph Campbell used the term *metaphor* when describing the purpose of myth, and if myths are to be taken metaphorically, then they don't have to be true or false, fact or fiction. They simply have to act as stories that represent or symbolize something else, which is what metaphors do. Therefore, the characters and events in a myth, religious story, or legend may be more about what they symbolize than they are about themselves directly. Thus, a God fighting a three-headed creature may not be so much about the God or the hydra, but more about overcoming huge challenges or standing up to obstacles and succeeding. A raging, angry God of the Sea unleashing a flood on lowly sinful humans may be less about the God, the flood, and the drowning people, and more about how karma catches up with us in the end, and how our actions have often equal and opposite reactions.

Like the stories in the Bible, myths can also be educational, moral, and inspirational—even motivational. They can entertain and instruct us, direct and guide us, and even tell us what to do to assure our success in the world. Magical and supernatural elements serve as story devices to represent the unknown both within us and outside of us. Everything is symbolic, and everything is important.

In other words, a myth or legend is a single story that tells two stories at once, as described so succinctly in "The Role of Truth in Myth—Myth As Metaphor" from the Exploring the Arts Foundation. What a great way to describe myth and legend. Two stories at once, two purposes, two truths on two different levels. Because although metaphor, symbol, and motif are ever present in all myths, we still see glimpses of hard fact, hard knowledge, and hard science—even if it looks a little funky to us on this side of the wormhole of time.

A Time of Gods

Take, for example, a couple of our favorite Roman Gods—Jupiter and Vulcan, to be exact. Jupiter is the supreme God of light and sky in the Roman pantheon, and the Roman equivalent to the Greek Zeus, also known as Jove (sounds similar to Jehovah!). Vulcan is the Roman God of fire and the patron of metal works and craftsmanship. His Greek equivalent is Hephaestus. Jupiter throws lightning bolts through the sky and was also called Totans, the Thunderer; Lucetius, of the light (similar to Lucifer); and Fulgurator (of lightning). Vulcan, on the other hand, had his workshop below the volcano Mt. Etna in Sicily, where he forged metals, iron, and armor that shook the ground and spewed ash and spark and flame into the skies above. Heck, his name even sounds like volcano.

So thousands of years ago, when there were raging thunderstorms and volcanic eruptions, without the scientific understanding of weather, climate, storm systems, volcanism, plate tectonics, and associated earthquakes, people did what they had to do to deal with nature in a way that made sense to them. Surely, those brutal storms and that fierce lightning that lit up the dark skies were the rage of a God disappointed in mortal actions. Surely, the shaking of the ground and the eruption of ash and debris out of the top of the mountain was the God below forging his wares, angry perhaps at his wife, Venus, who was a big flirt and desired by all.

The actions and behaviors of nature became the actions and behaviors of the characters in myth and religious stories.

In fact, what was going on in the skies was as much of interest as what was happening on the ground. Cosmic influences and even pure astronomical knowledge are evident in many myths and origin stories. Our ancestors were observers and had a keen sense of what was going on with the stars and planets and the moon, even if they didn't necessarily understand the hard science behind it all. Gods and Goddesses represented various planets and the sun and the moon. Solar deities became associated with some of the most critically important deities and even religious figures (Mithras, Jesus), and even the constellations were assigned to various deities.

The earliest sciences may have been astronomy and mathematics, with medicine coming up from the rear to show. Descriptions of the physical world and how it "measured up" are all over myths and religious texts, often peppered in with tales of fantastical and even miraculous elements, begging the question: Did our ancient ancestors have vivid imaginations as we do today, or was the supernatural world actually visible to them in a way it isn't today? Look at the popularity of the paranormal today. Can we really then discount all stories of oddities we don't have names or explanations for that our ancestors wrote and sang and spoke of?

We are not so sure.

The Mill and the Wheel

Because astronomy is a field of science that relies on observation, we today have the abundance of ancient glyphs, rock art, and drawings of the movement of the moon, sun, and stars, and even how they correspond with natural growing and hunting cycles below. Our calendars reflect this ancient astronomical knowledge of measuring time in accordance with cosmic movement and activity. Even the moon's phases and solar and lunar eclipses were easily recorded over periods of time if one was observant enough, even later allowing the Greek astronomer and mathematician Hipparchus to study and perfect our understanding of the phenomenon known as the precession of the Earth's axis as approximately 26,000 years about the second century BC, long before we had telescopes and computers to figure that stuff out for us.

One of the most instrumental written works examining myth and the transmission of knowledge is *Hamlet's Mill: An Essay Investigating the Origins of Human Knowledge and its Transmission Through Myth.* Published in 1969, and written by two scholars, professor of history and philosophy of science at M.I.T. Giorgio de Santillana and Hertha von Dechend, professor of the history of science at University of Frankfort, *Hamlet's Mill* was the amazing and complex examination of the role of astronomical objects and movements, and their association with various myths and legends. When others were theorizing about myth as a representation of a hero's journey and an archetypal human adventure story, the authors of this book contended that it was more about "as above, so below," and the connection between cosmic activities and those that happened far below, on earth.

The title came from the story of a legendary mythical figure called Amleth, who owned a powerful mill that rotated around the pole star. This heavenly mill's wheel, as the myth states, symbolizes the turning in the sky of the stars, and the axle of the wheel is the axis running from the North Pole. The Amleth myth has elements not found in the Shakespearean story of Hamlet, but our concern here is that this mill would become the great wheel in the sky by which astronomical events occurred. The spinning millstones then represented the circular rotation of the orbits of planets and our own as it spins on its axis, giving us our particular view of the skies.

The main astronomical observation this book focuses on is the precession of the equinox and the travels of the sun through our zodiac system. Because this would have been observable to all cultures and civilizations, the theory is that common themes in myths all over the world come from said observations, with the symbolic retelling of the sun's journey and the appearance of a new pole star, often accompanied by great earthy distress. The millstone would fall off its frame in the legend, signifying the passing of one zodiacal age giving way to another, which was later symbolized by tales of kings overthrown by new rulers and a new established order for the "new age." The stories of Gods and Goddesses and their own interactions with the sun, sky, sea, and earth were then to be thought of as imaginative ways to depict astronomical events, including comets, meteors, dying stars, and solar activity, but at the heart of it all was the precession.

The strange thing is, this precession took a total of 26,000 years for the sun to make a complete journey around the astrological cosmos from the point of view of our Earth's wobbling axis, and that means that observations would have to have taken place for thousands of years to figure this out. Somehow, these ancient peoples knew of the changes of one zodiac sign to another and often modeled their stories with symbols associated with one sign. The incredible focus on detail and observation of the skies above obviously played a huge role in the ancient worldview that emerged over time into the view we have today.

As the wheel of the mill continues to turn on and on, we pass from one age into the next, from one epoch into another, from one celestial cycle to another, and a number of books look at the precession as a model for many legends and myths, suggesting that science and math somehow wormed its way into those stories of gods and goddesses we once took for pure entertainment.

Though *Hamlet's Mill* was dissected, and not always positively so, by critics and scholars who blanched at the complex and often-confusing text and the numerous assumptions that were based upon a shaky and unproven theory of the existence of the discovery of the precession long before the acceptable Greek date, perhaps even as far back as 4000 BC, and despite the many suggestions that the two author/scholars were operating with limited, tenuous, and outdated source information, it has taken on a sort of renaissance as a more scientific way to examine myth, even as it goes against the grain of most scholarly thought. A whole new area of study has sprung out of *Hamlet's Mill* called "archeo-astronomy" (which we'll discuss in Chapter 7), and many books that came afterward, including the seminal *The Mythic Image* by Joseph Campbell, *Fingerprints of the Gods* by Graham Hancock, and dozens of others, attempted to either challenge, expand, confirm, or deny the book's content.

Interestingly, the rise of astronomy was often integral to religious ideas. In the Hindu Vedas, for example, we can find references to everything from the division of a year into 360 days of 12 equal parts, the actual creation of the Universe from a void or nothingness (pre–Big Bang!), and even the monthly calculations that would lay the groundwork for their astrological system, which varies from our own by one month and one sign. The ancient Vedic texts mention a spherical-shaped planet Earth (we thought this dang thing was flat long after the Hindu figured it out!). These calculations did not deny or defy their religious belief; they added credence to them.

Even the Old Testament hints at a scientific understanding of the Earth's position in the heavens, and its fixed place there. Even the rising and setting of the sun is mentioned (Ecclesiastes 1:5) in the same places each day and night, as well as the importance of sound and vibration and light as fundamental creative forces (Genesis). Even Job knew that the Earth hung in the sky on "nothing" (Job 26:7)! Call it a crude description of our gravitational position in the solar system, but he nailed it. Yet we have ongoing arguments today over the huge discrepancies in how old the earth is, how humans evolved, and even which gender came from which—all because of the paths that science and religion took throughout the course of thousands of years.

Still, for every connection, there was a big misconnection, as in the belief in the Old Testament of a flat earth, of being able to stop the sun in the sky, and of exactly where woman came from, and it surely was not a rib. So how do we find the fact in the fiction? Especially when we are given tantalizing examples of both? Maybe, as Joseph Campbell suggested of myth, the stories of the Bible were actually meant to be taken metaphorically. Two of the earliest church fathers, Origin (185–254 AD) and Augustine (354–430 AD), rejected the literal interpretation in favor of a more metaphorical and even mythical model. Yet even as myth or metaphor, we still have to wonder where this breach occurred. If you continue to observe your surroundings and note those observances, and as science and technology either support or refute them, knowledge should be unified. And yet, through time, knowledge became split between what could be proved in an empirical sense, and what was supposed to be the realm of faith and divine intervention. This rift exists to this day, making it very difficult, if not downright impossible, to focus on the common themes and motifs that suggest that at one point in time, we agreed.

A Tale of Nephilim
By Scotty Roberts

The phrase *going viral* is, of course, a modernism we use for the spread of information, be that information something of importance or just banal entertainment that has little to do with advancing humanity. In the case of the *Nephilim,* according to ancient Hebrew/Israelite mythology, that story had already run rampantly viral by the time we find any record of it in their religious documents. According to the accounts, the earth had been filled with the offspring of an intercoursive intermingling between the gods and humans, rendering the entirety of the human race "tainted" with non-human blood.

This story is mirrored in myriad accounts found throughout antiquity, from sprawling cultural mythologies to tribal legends. Nearly 600 different ancient versions of these mythological creatures exist, from the Hebrew Bible to the Tuatha de Danaan of the Celts; from the Chinese dragon to tales of Krishna and the Mayan's Quedtzlcoatl—to name just a small handful. But just how these tales spread with any sort of precision from ancient culture to ancient culture is a mystery to be unraveled. But one thing is certain: No matter the cultural tale, when you burn off all the dross, you are left with one, seemingly indisputable common thread: The interruption of the bloodlines of the human race.

With the advance of civilization and its spread from pockets of established places of origin, humanity spread out and carried with them the ancient stories told and retold again and again, with new twists and variants added to build the newer version of the mythology in the rising, newer religions. But perspective alters the understanding of how these things transmitted: Archaeologists and anthropologists would call this the equaniminous evolution of civilized culture, whereas alternative theorists might simply interpret such similarities in cultural mythologies as humanity's exposure to outside elements that influenced change.

There is, however, one ancient symbol that seems to piggyback the story of this "race interrupted," and that is the symbol of the serpent, found in nearly every ancient culture. From the story of human origins found in the Hebrew religion's Book of Genesis, we find the "serpent character" tempting the mother of all humanity. On a closer examination of the language, we learn that the eating of "forbidden fruit" is merely a cultural, encoded cover story for a much greater event of seduction and impregnation by a god who is later equated with a serpent character. When you examine the linguistics and etymology of the ancient story, it has it foundational moorings in the accounts of the Sumerian culture's pantheon of gods, the Annunaki. Elil/Enlil, the chief god of the Annunaki, charges his brother god, Enki/Ea, with the creation of "primeval man" as a slave race to conduct the work of the gods. After time, the humans, seeking freedom, gain the aid of their creator, Enki/Ea, to lead them in rebellion against Elil/Enlil. Enki/Ea is associated with the "Serpent's Marsh," which became known as "Ea's Den"—or "Ea-den/Eden" found in the adapted Hebrew text of the similar creation/rebellion event.

The story of the serpent character in Genesis' Garden of Eden is adapted information from the much older Sumerian account. In the case of the Garden of Eden's serpent character, the transfer of religious mythology from one ancient mooring to the next was carried out by Moses, the founder of Judaism. When he wrote his Book of Genesis, he had already been raised in the courts of 18th dynasty Egypt, and was thoroughly immured in ancient Egyptian mysticism and magical religious practice for the first 40 years of his life. The next 40 years he was married to the daughter of the pagan high priest of Midian and learning the Sinatic religions, along with the ancient Canaanite, Syrian, and Sumerian religious mythologies. Without a doubt, the transfer of ancient cultural and religious mythology to the foundational building blocks of Hebraic religion demonstrates just one culture's perpetuation of a viral mythology. The Hebrew story of the Nephilim is built upon the more ancient tale of Enki/Ea rising from the Serpent's Marsh (Ea's Den). The hand of the gods in the creation, proliferation, and interruption of human bloodlines, as well as the delivery of the forbidden knowledge of the gods leading to rebellion against the chief god is a commonality in these ancient accounts.

One step further in this particular analysis: Elil of the Sumerians becomes El of the Hebrews, rendering as El, Elohim, El Shaddai, and ElElyon, whereas Enki/Ea becomes Yaweh, the Hebrew word for Jehovah.

The bottom line is that perspective and interpretation of these ancient mythologies are the keys to understanding how they spread from culture to culture. In my travels in Egypt with Dr. John Ward, what I saw throughout Egypt was the overwhelming proliferation of ancient symbolism in art, iconography, and language all having immense bearing on the hermetic and esoteric knowledge behind the spread and proliferation of the story of the Nephilim, beginning with the Egyptian tale of the descent of the Ogdod to the creation mound near Menindat Habu to the ancient Sumerian Annunaki who bred primeval humanity.

In and throughout all is the symbol of the serpent that appears as the constant element throughout human history to carry the message of a race created, enslaved, and interrupted. And this mythology—when you dig for its encoded underpinnings—reveals a story that spread through all of humanity's ancient cultural myths and legends.

Scotty Roberts is the publisher of Intrepid Magazine *and the founder of the Paradigm Symposium. He has authored three books with New Page Books:* The Rise and Fall of the Nephilim, The Secret History of the Reptilians, *and* The Exodus Reality *(coauthored with Dr. John Ward). He is also the author and illustrator of* The Rollicking Adventures of Tam O'Hare. *Scotty lives with his wife and children in rural Wisconsin.*

Literal Truths?

Maybe it was scriptural literalism that tripped us up, or maybe it was a move away from the fantastical to the more down to earth as we began to understand that there wasn't some guy up in the clouds tossing lightning bolts around, and that thunder and lightning and rain were natural events that were the result of some meteorological brew we were only beginning to get the right ingredients for. As belief moved away from observation and empirical experience to more inward reflection and personal subjectivity, we may have become divided between what we knew for fact and what we knew on faith, and the two got thrown together like chocolate and peanut butter, or maybe oil and water. They didn't always mix or go well together.

Just as archeology seeks to understand our history through the recovery of remains of the past civilizations, biblical archeology seeks the same with focus on finding evidence for or against stories in the Old Testament and New Testament and the evolution of the Judeo-Christian cosmogony. It gives structure and fleshes out the stories with factual evidence of who these people were and how they lived. We look to the past to understand our present, and how we got here, while also seeking to discern factual knowledge from fictional inspiration. Herschel Shanks, the editor of *Biblical Archeology Review,* writes in "What Brings You Here?" (July/August 2013): "Many people are interested in biblical archeology because it fleshes out the Biblical world for them. It makes the Bible come alive as a real world and not only a text grounded in faith." This field, he continues, offers glimpses into the homes they lived in, the pots they cooked with, and how they lit their lamps in the dark—all of the big and small factors that allow us to peer through the window of time and "feel the sweep of humanity of which you are a part."

The general study of symbol and myth offers us a window to the past, but a fragmented one, according to Laird Scranton, author of several books on symbolism, cosmology, and the African Dogon, who had a very sophisticated scientific understanding, and shared many traits and traditions with ancient Egyptians and even Hebrews. Scranton writes in *Comparative Cosmology: The Dogon, Buddhism and Ancient Egypt,* that the way we can overcome these fragments and gaps in evidence of the past is by looking at the "parallel nature of myth and symbol in different cultures." Scranton comments that these similarities are striking and may have involved more unconventional means of transmission from one culture to another, possibly even involving the use of archetypes and "innate psychology as a credible way to explain their near-global appearance." In an excerpt from his book *The Cosmological Origins of Myth and Symbol,* Scranton also writes that "when we study the actual creation traditions of distant cultures, uniqueness of view is not what we typically find. Rather, what we see instead is an almost predictive commonality of theme, symbol and storyline, expressed in distinctly similar terms and organized according to a set of familiar states of creation." Might these parallels reflect a "vision of ancient cosmology as a kind of instructed system of civilization, one that was typically associated with knowledgeable ancestor/teachers or beneficent ancestor/Gods?" We will explore this and other theories of how this knowledge was transmitted in a later chapter, as well as the idea of a "common parent cosmology," as Scranton calls it, that may explain all these common elements, which then leads to the quest to discover what this parent cosmology is—and where it came from.

Myth, legend, religious stories, cosmogenesis stories, cultural narratives—all are ways and means of conveying the attempts of our ancestors to figure out who they were, how they got here, and what was going on around them when the skies shook and the ground shuddered and plants died and were born anew, and the sun and the moon rose and set and rose again, sometimes different, and the stars moved across the sky in patterns and shapes.

In his seminal work, *Fingerprints of the Gods,* Graham Hancock looks at myth, most notably end of the world or cataclysmic myth, as a valid means of information, and information we must listen to, no matter the form it comes in:

> The possession of a conscious, articulated history is one of the faculties that distinguishes human beings from animals. Unlike rats, say, or sheep, or cows, or pheasants, we have a past, which

is separate from ourselves. We therefore have the opportunity, as I have said, to learn from the experiences of our predecessors. Is it because we are perverse, or misguided, or simply stupid that we refuse to recognize those experiences unless they have come down to us in the form of bona fide "historical records"? And is it arrogance or ignorance which leads us to draw an arbitrary line separating "history" from "prehistory" at about 5000 years before the present—defining the records of "history" as valid testimony and the records of "prehistory" as primitive delusions? At this stage in a continuing investigation, my instinct is that we may have put ourselves in danger by closing our ears for so long to the disturbing ancestral voices which reach us in the form of myths. This is more an intuitive than a rational feeling, but it is by no means unreasonable.

By looking at what Hancock calls the fingerprints of these ancient geniuses that composed such myths, and the amazing evidence they left behind in the form of the advanced calendric systems of the Mayans, or the complex edifices of the Pyramids, he cannot disregard what these "Newtons and Shakespears and Einsteins of the last Ice Age" where trying to tell us: "Yes, they were saying, *'Kilroy was here.'* And, yes, they found an ingenious way to tell us when they were here. Of these things I have no doubt." And whether their myths were of worlds ending, or worlds beginning, we owe it to ourselves to stop, look, and listen.

Our lives are told in the stories we tell. Sometimes those stories are personal to our tribe, or to us, and sometimes they are universal. All contain nuggets of truth that we will then pass down to our future generations, through the stories we tell ourselves today.

Once Upon a Time:
Story, Lore, and Legend

I love studying folklore and legends. The stories
that people passed down for a thousand years
without any sort of marketing support are obviously
saying something appealing about the basic human
condition.

—Tim Schafer

If you take myth and folklore, and these things
that speak in symbols, they can be interpreted in so
many ways that although the actual image is clear
enough, the interpretation is infinitely blurred, a sort
of enormous rainbow of every possible colour you
could imagine.

—Diana Wynne Jones

What I find interesting about folklore is the dialogue
it gives us with storytellers from centuries past.

—Terri Windling

We have always been story-tellers. From the dawn of humankind,
we've been constructing ideas of who we are, how we got here, and

what our purpose is, as well as attempting to describe, through creative and imaginative means, how the world around us just might work. Before science, there was story, and in a sense, science has always been embedded in stories throughout time, as well as knowledge, wisdom, and truth.

Once upon a time, we didn't have the means to send a piece of information across the globe at lightning speed. We had to find other ways to convey what we were thinking. Around the fire perhaps we sat, speaking in whispered tones as we told tales and did our best to describe the world, as we knew it, even if we didn't have a clue as to how to understand it. The reality around us was so vast, so bizarre, and so utterly incomprehensible, and we did not yet have the scientific savvy or acumen to understand any of it.

But we had words—and images. And we had stories.

Stories in Writing

Whether in the form of images on a wall of rock, or words to a breathless audience, or in writing, stories provided not just a form of entertainment to pass the time, but a way of expressing ideas and information via the vehicle of a three-act dramatic structure embellished with imaginative add-ons. The oldest stories may have been those out of ancient Mesopotamia, such as the epic tales of Gilgamesh etched into clay and carved onto stone pillars about 700 BC, changing from generation to generation and perhaps even becoming a part of future stories. Gilgamesh, according to Dr. Michael Lockett in *The Basics of Storytelling*, contained elements such as a garden and a flood, which may have later morphed into the Old Testament's Book of Genesis.

Lockett also tells us that story-telling in written form was utilized by ancient Egyptians, in the form of the Westcar Papyrus. Possibly the sons of Cheops, the builder of the great Pyramid that bears his name, entertained their father with such stories of magic and heroism. The tales of Aesop, a slave who told stories and fables that survive to this day, although claimed by the Greek as having originated with them, may have instead come to us from some part of North Africa, set in writing about 300 BC–250 BC. "Storytelling has helped adults pass on wisdom, knowledge, and culture through the generations before they were finally printed in written form," Lockett writes, citing the great epics of the Greek Homer from 1200 BC, that were not written down until 700 BC and became the *Odyssey* and the *Iliad* we know of today.

We discussed in Chapter 1 the importance of oral tradition as a means of passing on generational stories of individuals, families, events, and even what life was like for those who came before us. Oral history and tradition were eventually recorded not just in audio form, but later, when writing systems developed and evolved, as written text, to assure its continued preservation.

Eventually, some of those oral stories took on a folkloric element when these otherwise eyewitness accounts of real events and real people were reinterpreted on an ongoing basis, each time adding on new aspects of the original story until the end result contained only a grain of historical accuracy. Not all, but many of the oral stories our ancestors once told, became the stuff of legend and of lore by losing some of their historical perspective in favor of lavish and imaginative fantasy. Even values and religious rituals changed the historical nature of the original event, and often became more important than the event itself.

Parables and Fables

We also have so many parables, defined as a usually short fictitious story that illustrates a moral attitude or a religious principle. Parables are not based upon historical events, but convey a deeper truth about how an individual or a group should behave. Using fiction to drive home a moral is something many parents know works well with small children, who seem to respond to the combination, just as we respond, perhaps subconsciously, to parables and to fables, which are entirely fictional and often magical or fantastical stories that are meant to convey a truth, a moral, or a specific theme.

The most famous fables of all are the talking animal stories of an ancient Greek slave who lived between 620 BC and 560 BC, and who may or may not have told hundreds of brief stories that were meant not just to entertain, but also to teach greater truths than actual, specific ones. These stories became known as "Aesop's Fables" or the "Aesopica" credited to Aesop, although most modern scholars agree he did not create them all. These fables all had a specific formula: They were short, fictitious, were useful to life, contained talking creatures and plants that were often given human qualities, and featured very little human to human interactions. They usually began with an introduction, followed by the story, and ended with a moral. Some had political meanings, some were values-oriented, and some were based on existing proverbs. To this day, Aesop's Fables are being retold and reinterpreted.

Fables are found in every culture and every country, and originally were used as training exercises for prose and public speaking competitions in ancient Greek and Roman education systems. More modern fables include the popular children's story "Bambi," written in 1923 by Felix Salten and later Disney-fied into the classic animated motion picture, and even George Orwell's political satire *Animal Farm,* the 1945 classic that used animals to tell a story of Stalinist Communism and totalitarianism.

Märchen Und Sagen

The term *Märchen Und Sagen* is used by folklorists to describe the two main categories of oral tales, and could also apply to written tales as well. *Märchen* can be translated into English as "fairy tale" or "little stories" that are not intended as truth and often occur in entirely fantastical settings with utterly magical and sometimes supernatural elements like trolls, fairies, and poison apples. *Sagen* describes what we would call legends, which are stories of a particular event that occurred at a particular time and place, and may or may not include embellishments such as supernatural interferences or magical elements.

As with myth and religion, story-telling used specific themes as a foundation for representing a particular universal truth, even an archetypal or a psychological one. Many of the same themes present in myth, which includes the hero's journey, made their way into historical narratives and became the stuff of "sagen," or legends.

Legends

No matter what form story-telling took on, the purpose was to pass on information, because even the most imagination-based fiction has seeds of truth that can help us, thousands of years later, identify key characteristics of a culture and their way of life. Legends are often described as stories of historical events that are not meant to be symbolic narrative, as some other forms of story-telling, such as myths, are. Legends specifically are often based upon core truths that are embellished upon over time, such as the King Arthur tales or the stories of Robin Hood, Paul Bunyon, Lady Godiva, Romulus and Remus, and others—eventually becoming more "fictionalized" over time and therefore losing some of their weight as actual legend. The Brothers Grimm (whom we will talk more about) describe legends as "historically grounded folktales" and modern folklorists recognize them as historical narratives that contain folk beliefs and experiences indigenous to the culture telling them, and filled with the symbolism and traditional values of that culture. It is that specific cultural spin that makes legends so hard to dissect when looking for solid factual information, yet legends may indeed be telling us about important events that actually transpired.

The word *legend* comes from the Old French *legende,* from the Medieval Latin *legenda,* meaning a narrative of an event. A legend can be about a person, as described previously; or a place, such as Atlantis or Shangri-La; or even a creature, such as Nessie the Loch Ness Monster or Bigfoot. Even an inanimate object can become a legend. Think the Holy Grail, the fountain of youth, the Philosopher's Stone, and the Emerald Tablets. The original use of the word implied a fictional content, but in time, people began to adopt the term as a literary narrative of a possibly historical event, much in the way folk tales became.

The problem with looking for truth in legend is the passage of time, as well as the interpretive assaults by generations of story-tellers who add their own touches to the original tale, just as we today embellish actual stories of events that have occurred in our own lives. (Come on. Was that first kiss in kindergarten really *that* amazing that you saw stars and unicorns dancing in the air? Or is it just more fun to remember it that way?)

❧

The Anatomy of a Legend

One of the most popular and enduring legends of all time is that of a man who led his country into battle against the evil Saxons and led the Knights of the Round Table on the quest for the Holy Grail: King Arthur. The legend of the Arthurian king has gone through so many changes and transformations through time, but there was an origin point, and it may have been a real king that started it all, or at least a real historical figure involved in the Saxon invasion. The story goes that Arthur was a British leader who led his country against Saxon invaders in the early part of the sixth century. Arthur was also the head of a group of very special knights that made up the Round Table, including the almost equally legendary Sir Percival and Sir Lancelot, in the quest to find the cup of Christ, the Holy Grail—which is *also* a legend, because some say it was the cup that Christ's blood spilled into when he was pierced with a spear while on the cross, and others say it is the chalice used at the Last Supper. Arthur was married to the stunning Queen Guinevere, also a legend in her own right, as was her torrid and forbidden romance with Lancelot. Guiding Arthur in his legendary 12 battles and his more spiritual quests was *another* legend, Merlin the Magician. Arthurian legend also includes a magical sword called Excalibur, and an equally magical and legendary burial place for this king at an island called Avalon. Oh, and then there's Mordred, the legendary son of Arthur and his own half-sister, the evil Morganna. Mordred is said to have mortally wounded his own father in the final Battle of Camlann.

Interestingly, most of that story angle was added on by 12th-century-AD French poet and writer Chrétien de Troyes, who created many of these elements by adding characters and events that ultimately created the genre of Arthurian and chivalric romance of medieval literature, which was a form of poem or verse narrative that spoke of adventures of knights and heroes on a quest, intended for aristocratic audiences. But before he got hold of the story, Geoffrey of Monmouth had already created his own Arthur angle in his 12th-century *Historia Regum Britanniae* (*History of the Kings of Britain*). There were also already in existence some Welsh and Breton epic poems and stories that spoke of Arthur, a great warrior defending Britain from both human and supernatural enemies.

And before that, there were many mentions of a celebrated Romano-British leader who fought against the invading Saxons and may indeed have engaged in 12 battles, culminating in the legendary Battle at Mount Badon, during which Arthur is said to have killed more than 900 men singlehandedly.

While scholars and historians continue to argue over whether Arthur actually was a king who led his men into battle and his knights into chivalrous adventures, or maybe a Celtic folk deity, or even a re-telling of the Christ myth, complete with 12 "disciples," or just a really amazing warrior who fought like hell and had stories told about him, the story continues to engage modern audiences today in the forms of movies, TV shows, novels, and non-fiction books that attempt to answer the question: Who was King Arthur?

Many legends follow this trajectory of beginning with a seed that may have historical accuracy, but is then planted and then pulled up and replanted over and over again until the final fruit results in a completely reinterpreted telling of what was once a true story. We, the present generation, are left with the task of finding the fact within the fiction.

The role legends played in providing cultural and historical information about a specific person, thing, or event continues to this day, even with our more fantastical and often viral urban legends.

Urban Legends

Today's contemporary legends often go by the name "urban legend," although an urban setting is not required to qualify as such. These modern myths and legends often originate with a true event, such as a deadly spider bite, but then go viral because of technology and social networking, all the while taking on new life and a whole lot of fiction along the way. Often changes are made because of regional beliefs, and some urban legends actually do accurately portray aspects of modern life, such as the fear of something or the danger of something else. These modern-day cautionary tales are meant to instill fear, and even sometimes panic and horror, as part of their propagation.

The scarier they are, the faster and wider they spread.

The first known use of the term *urban legend* in the general public comes from the publication of a series of popular books by an English professor at the University of Utah named Jan Harold Brunvand. The books were a collection of legends compiled and released to the general public under the title *The Vanishing Hitchhiker: American Urban Legends and Their Meanings* in 1981. The purpose of these stories was to show that legend and even folklore were not exclusive to primitive and ancient cultures, and that we could actually glean some understanding and knowledge about our own modern culture by studying these stories.

Interestingly, most urban legends involve stories that are said to have happened to "a friend of a friend" (FOAF) and are rarely traceable to one actual person. Sometimes, we can trace these stories to a source, as in the Lovers' Lane murders in Texarkana in 1946, resulting in the urban legend "The Hook" or "The Hookman," a serial killer with a hook for one hand that allegedly killed lovers while they were necking in their cars in remote places, and left his hook stuck to the side of their car door handle. Some variations apply!

Most urban legends we hear about today, especially via social networking on the Internet, are just made-up stories, jokes, hoaxes, and pranks intended to spread like wildfire and cause people to freak out, which they often do, despite an obvious lack of any real details by which the story might be proven true. This goes to show us just how easy it is to spread false information when fear is at the core of it—and explains why the most memorable urban legends involve heinous crimes, bizarre and enigmatic creatures, or specific locations that must be avoided at all costs! These narratives, also referred to as "urban belief stories," speak of a collective belief in a specific location that are alleged to be true accounts, even if they utilize the FOAF device, and end up spreading orally, with or without embellishment. They become urban myths that live on long after the initial people involved have died.

Some of the darkest urban legends involve entities that stalk and kill human beings—entities that may or may not be the stuff of pure fiction. Here are a few to keep in mind and avoid if you actually do see them: (Check out *http://creepypast.wikia.com* for more of these stories!)

Slenderman—A mysterious entity often depicted as being tall and thin, wearing a black suit with a white shirt and necktie, and having a blank face. If he stares at you, you die. He is often found lurking in the woods or around children.

The Rake—A strange humanlike creature that allegedly began appearing in summer 2003 in parts of the northeastern United States, primarily rural New York. The creature traumatized some witnesses, although most people believe this urban legend was designed entirely for fun and games and public gullibility.

The Ghost Car—Police in Garden City, Georgia, apparently engaged in a wild goose chase with a ghost car that could drive through fences. The white car was allegedly caught on video and posted on the Internet.

Bloody Mary—No, not the drink, but the creepy woman named Mary Worth who allegedly appears in the mirror if you chant her name three times in the dark or by candlelight. She wants, it seems, her reflection back, which she was prevented from seeing after a disfiguring accident, or so the legend goes. (Coauthor Marie tried this many times as a child with slumber party friends. The only person who appeared in the mirror was her mom telling her and her friends they were nuts!)

There are those who firmly believe they have encountered these monsters and mysteries out of place and time, and there are those who insist they are nothing more than made-up stories Photoshopped or videotaped and put up on YouTube and various Websites to go viral, thus leading to more "sightings" and more questions. As long as these stories have some semblance of plausibility, or a few vague details thrown in for good measure, there will be some people who will not only believe them, but also perpetuate them by taking them viral.

By the way, as an aside, one of the most popular Halloween costumes in the last few years is the Slenderman. Good marketing or spooky truth?

❀

A Storyteller Speaks
By Elana Freeland

The old myths, legends, and fairy tales are really not about what we think of as "facts" but about being human. Even the gods in the great myths (Greek, Scandinavian, Nordic, etc.) have very human traits. The same themes play over and over in the myths of every culture: the gods are fascinated by human beings but want them to remain subservient, while the humans want to be the most human possible, which means *moral*. Thus the gods have power, but not morality, and the human being is always struggling between good and evil, which is what makes the ancient tales riveting to this very day, the struggle for truth being greater than obtaining factual information.

Which brings up a second question: "Why might fiction be a better conveyor of truth than fact?" Ancient myths, legends, and fairy tales are fiction in the sense that they're not *exactly* nonfiction—in exactly the same sense that biographies are not exactly nonfiction. These stories are the biographies of all of humanity told in different cultural voices. Greek myths differ from Mesopotamian myths because the epochs portrayed are as different as the peoples and times they portray.

For decades, I have told hundreds of these tales hundreds of times to big and small groups, old and young. Whereas a *fact* is a mere reflection of a tiny bit of reality, the storyteller's voice draws everyone into a total reality—a dream reality that deals morally with the reality of being human. Perhaps this is why storytellers were also the teachers, shamans, and priests: Their capacity to induct people into a world otherwise inaccessible except through dreams, initiation, and death.

Rudolf Steiner included a vast mythology curriculum in his Waldorf educational system which is based upon the phylogeny-recapitulates-ontogeny process that every young person must travel in order to truly mature. Steiner perceived that the youth's present incarnation needs to spend just a bit of time in the consciousness of the past: first the archetypal fairy tale, then the fable, then the legend, and finally the grand myth, until at last, the youth stands at the door of history. Is history "factual"? Yes, but in the same way myths, legends, and fairy tales are "factual." *They are all points of view.* Sadly, to our spiritual poverty, these vehicles of imagining and feeling what it is to be human have been shunted off into distorting Disney cartoons while corporate television and film screenwriters have usurped the role of cultural storytellers.

Elana Freeland is a story-teller, mythologist, and writer who lied and confabulated as an only child, then as an adult learned to tell myths, legends, and fairytales during her training to be a Waldorf teacher. She started the Seattle Storytelling Guild and the Olympia Storytellers Guild, and has taught mythology and story-telling through the University of Washington and Evergreen State College. Besides telling stories professionally for a decade, she told and read stories and poems on her three-and-a-half-year KAOS-FM program, "The Round Table." She recently completed writing her Sub Rosa America *series, a fictional history of America since the Kennedy assassination told from the vantage point of a multitude of stories during a journey along Route 66.*

Appleseed Stories

A perfect example of truth-based legend is the story of John Chapman, born in Leominster, Massachusetts, on September 26, 1774, and better known to the American public as "Johnny Appleseed." Chapman was a skilled nurseryman who spent 50 years of his life growing apple trees and supplying apple seeds to pioneers in the midwestern United States. Chapman gave away and sold many trees. He owned a number of nurseries in the region, including Ohio, Pennsylvania, Kentucky, Illinois, and Indiana, and, as the legend has it, was very successful but lived very simply. He was a very religious man, and his generosity, along with his conservation efforts and the catchy nickname, made him a living legend. Possible embellishments to his legend suggest that as Johnny traveled, he wore his cooking pot on his head as a hat. Chapman also allegedly sang a traveling song or Swedenborgian hymn, everywhere he went, which is still sung before meals in some American households today: "Oooooh, the Lord is good to me, and so I thank the Lord, for giving me the things I need, the sun and the rain and the apple seed. The Lord is good to me. Amen, Amen, Amen, Amen, Amen."

Johnny Appleseed has entered the entertainment lexicon with children's stories, a movie, a Broadway play, and numerous cartoons, and festivals are held all over the country in his honor. Appleseed was a real living legend, probably far more normal and less eccentric than some elements of his legend suggest, and no doubt as time goes on, his story will be embellished even further. Yet at its core, is historical fact.

American Folk Legends
By S.E. Schlosser

My double-great-grandfather, Richard Johnson, was a Pennsylvania Dutch hex doctor. Yes, you read that right. A real-life hex doctor who achieved quite a bit of fame in eastern Pennsylvania. People were carried into his office with badly broken legs and walked out again on their own two feet, completely healed. Legends are still told about the man more than a hundred years later. In fact, I met a Pennsylvania couple while hiking in Yellowstone last summer (2012) who knew all the Richard Johnson legends, which are still being told in their hometown.

When I was researching my book *Spooky Pennsylvania,* I interviewed a senior citizen who knew Richard Johnson. As a young child, she went with her mother to consult the hex doctor when conventional medicine failed to heal her fever-stricken infant sister. The senior citizen's body shook as she recalled how Richard Johnson prayed and chanted over the infant, smoke rising from his gloved hands, which clutched red-hot coals designed to draw the fever out of the tiny baby. The terrifying scene was still branded on her memory 70 years later, because she thought the baby would die. But the infant was fever-free by the time the family reached home, and today is a grandmother herself.

By definition, a legend is a traditional tale that is passed down from earlier times and believed to have its basis in historical fact. An example would be George Washington, who is the hero of many legends. My favorite is a tale collected for *Spooky New Jersey* in which the general's life was save by the ghost of a little girl during the first winter of the Revolutionary War, when Washington was headquartered in Morristown, New Jersey. Another George Washington legend is told at Gettysburg, where the general's ghost appeared to the stricken soldiers on Little Round Top and led the Northern charge against the Confederate Army, which threatened to destroy the unity of his beloved country.

Reaching back to Colonial times, the legend of Ocean-Born Mary (collected for *Spooky New England*) arose from a factual incident in which the dashing pirate Don Pedro spared the life of an Irish immigrant woman who had just given birth to a baby girl. The legend claims that the pirate kept track of the beautiful infant as she grew and came courting when Mary reached adulthood. Ocean-Born Mary's ghost is still said to haunt the New Hampshire house, which she shared with her reformed pirate.

A pre-Colonial legend that fascinates me was passed through many generations of a Native American tribe living in Washington State. In the tale, recounted in *Spooky Washington*, a very special man comes to live with the tribe for a year before "perishing" and being laid to rest on a rock above the tribal grounds. Eyewitnesses described a bright ship descending from the heavens and glowing figures retrieving the "body" from the rock. An ancient UFO legend?

I will close with a British Columbia myth from *Spooky Canada*, defined as a myth because it is an ancient story that deals with one of the great heroes of the Kaska First Nations. In this story, a monster called a "tix" attacks the camp of a wandering warrior and his wife. The warrior is killed by the monster, but the wife escapes with her baby and is chased across a frozen lake by the tix. The hero, Bladder-Head Boy, lives on an island with his people and destroys the stalking monster before it can harm anyone else. Why—you may ask—am I so fascinated by this particular story? Because, my friends, a "tix" is a wooly mammoth!

S.E. Schlosser is the author of the 26-book "Spooky Series" (Globe Pequot Press) and the publisher of the world-renowned, award-winning folklore site Americanfolklore.net.

Folklore and Folk Tales

Like legends, folklore often involves actual true historical events, or true personal experiences, but in general is much more fictional and designed to convey a specific message about a community of "folks" and how they view the world. The word *folk* refers to a group of people who share a common factor, such as familial connections, the same community, an occupation, religious beliefs, or language and culture. Folklore originated as a means of communication and expression for these groups, and according to Alan Dundes, the man most accredited with making folklore a valid academic field of study, in *Interpreting Folklore,* "No group of people, however remote or however simple their technology, has ever been discovered which does not employ some form of folklore. Because of this and because the same tales and proverbs may be known to both, folklore is a bridge between literate and non-literate societies."

Dundes, who was a folklorist at University of California, Berkeley, and the author of more than a dozen books, is often credited as the person behind making sure that folklore was considered a valid academic discipline. He himself received a PhD in folklore from Indiana University, and then went on to teach at both the University of Kansas and then at Berkeley, where he taught for 42 years until his death in 2005. His books covered almost every aspect of folklore, fables, oral and written literature, and even folkloric humor, and include *Interpreting Folklore; Bloody Mary in the Mirror: Essays in Psychoanalytic Folkloristics; When You're Up to Your Ass in Alligators: More Urban Folklore from the Paperwork Empire;* and *Fables of the Ancients?: Folklore in the Qur'an,* among other academic and popular titles.

Dundes understood that the most common method of transmission for folklore was oral and that this oral tradition, even if it was eventually written down later, was the backbone of true folk tales and the main criteria by which they were judged. Something purely written down was not necessarily true folklore, but based upon the original oral story. Folklore could include any oral form, including epic poems, myths, legends, fables, riddles, songs, jokes, nursery rhymes, toasts, insults, fairytales, and prayers, and even some non-verbal forms, like games, quilting, festivals and rituals, and symbols, could be considered in the realm of folklore.

We might be a little more accepting today of written forms of folklore, especially with the Internet as the most popular form of information transmission, and therefore a mainly written one, but true folklore has an artistic, structured form, despite ongoing alterations and additions made as the story is told and handed down.

The functions of folklore in culture and community are to validate that culture or community and to lay down a foundation of moral codes and values, but also to give a sense of group/communal existence to those sharing in the lore of their region. These tales of both fact and fantasy may also serve to give people a sense of largesse, or grandeur to boost the collective ego, although in more cases it seems folk tales serve as a communal glue. We can all think of modern folk tales, as with urban legends, that might have arisen right out our childhood communities, that we carry with us the rest of our lives and even pass on to our offspring.

Sometimes folklore and legend blend into a form of story-telling that depicts an extraordinary situation, person, or event as if it were actual historical fact. These stories tend to be oral in origin, and though the details of the setting and the times may be very accurate, there may be a bit of added on fabrication. Think of the most popular folk legends in America, with our stories of Paul Bunyan and Davy Crockett.

Folk legends have been categorized into four groups according to American folklorist Dr. Jan Harold Brunvand:

1. Religious legends of miracles, prayers answered, iconic appearances of religious figures, revelations.

2. Supernatural legends of ghosts, vampires, zombies, werewolves, and fairies, etc.

3. Personal legends of bigger-than-life real people like Billy the Kid and Johnny Appleseed.

4. Local legends that focus on a specific geographic area and history.

Even bad guys can achieve folk-legend status, as told in the tales of Billy the Kid, Jesse James, and Buffalo Bill, among others. Interestingly, most folk legends focus on the lives of men; few women seem fit to achieve that status of importance, although Annie Oakley and Lizzie Borden come to mind!

What the Old Wives Say

Never swallow your chewing gum! It takes seven years to pass through your system. Oh, and do *not,* under any circumstances, masturbate or you will go blind and grow hair on your palms! And for God's sake, stop making that awful face or your face will permanently stay that way! Now get away from the TV set because if you sit too close, your eyesight will fail.

Really, you can try any of these and chances are you'll be just fine. Thanks to a form of urban legend called "old wives' tales," we get all kinds of moral warnings that have absolutely no basis in fact. These tales originated as a part of the oral tradition of story-telling and were often used by mothers to keep their children in line. Though they seem like nasty warnings, the original intent may have been simple wisdom women hoped to pass on to make the lives of their children easier and fraught with fewer problems to contend with. (Who wants to grow up with hairy palms?)

Today, we have Websites like Google and Snopes and TV shows like *Mythbusters* to disprove these claims, but we most likely are creating some falsities of our own to pass on to future generations. Now stop lying, or you'll get white spots on your fingernails. And put down that chocolate. Don't you know it leads to acne?

When the Bough Breaks

One of the greatest folklorists in the history of the field is Sir James Frazer, the author of the seminal collection of folklore and mythology, focusing on nature rites, rituals, and celebrations, *The Golden Bough*. *Time* called this book one of the most influential books of the 20th century, and even today it is the standard by which we examine the way nature was once feared, worshipped, and revered, and how magic was present in the everyday lives of our primitive ancestors. Those ancestors, Frazer documents, emerged from a more "primitive" way of looking at the natural world around them into a more sophisticated culture through sympathetic magic and spiritual values that were, at one time, based upon more crude and even bloody and violent codes of behavior.

The cycle of birth, life, death, and rebirth is the backbone of Frazer's work, which goes into painstaking detail of the legends, myths, and rituals of cultures across the globe who were attempting to reconcile the natural world around them with their growing need for morals, ethics, and a connectedness to the larger cycle they were enmeshed in. Frazer, a Scottish anthropologist who lived between 1854 and 1941, first published two volumes of the *Bough* (named after a painting by J.M.W. Turner of a sacred tree in a sacred grove) in 1890, three more in 1900, and additional volumes in 1906–1915, and new essays have been added to more current volumes since. It's a heavy, hefty book, filled with comparative studies in myth, religion, ritual, and belief that focus on such primitive, even pagan, rites and rituals involving fertility, death, resurrection, human sacrifice, and the dying God. These themes, among others, were prevalent among what may have been fertility cults revolving around a "sacred king," and even have some commonalities, as discussed earlier, with the myths of Mithras, Christ, Dionysus, and even King Arthur. In fact, upon the book's release in England, a scandal erupted at the inclusion of the Christ story of Jesus' resurrection and similar "resurrection-themed" stories of a sacred deity, and the pagan origins of many of them, something the Christian church wasn't too keen on exposing!

Frazer's belief was that humanity progressed through several modes of thought and belief, from magical to religious to scientific. The more modern the times, the more knowledge available, thus taking what was once purely magical into the realms of actual scientific understanding as nature reveals more truths. Though the book was in a sense a tome about religion and the history of religious belief from primitive nature-based rites to the more theological elements of modern times, we could get an amazing glimpse into our historical past and how our ancestors once viewed the natural world of plants, animals, the sun, cycles of growing and harvest, and our own place in that world, which at the time appeared as magical. In fact, the *Bough* might be considered a manual of the history of sympathetic magic and ritual designed to mimic on earth the activities of the heavens, thus the "as above, so below" feel of many primitive nature rites. Frazer states that this "like produces like" also suggests that effects resemble their cause. He considers sympathetic magic one of two branches of magic our ancestors believed in when dealing with nature (think cave art and drawings of men successfully hunting prey for food). The other branch was contagious magic, which proceeds upon the notion that things which have once been conjoined must remain afterward, even when quite disserved from each other, in such a sympathetic relation that whatever is done to one must similarly affect the other.

Let us stop here for a moment and allow the shivers that just went up our collective spines to subside—shivers we felt because of this simple definition, and how much it mirrors the definition of quantum entanglement, where two particles that have once been in any form of contact, even when separated over vast distances, continue to influence and affect the other's behavior or "spin."

As above, so below.

Contagious Magic

Contagious magic also suggested, as many primitive and pagan rites show, that something that once was a part of the human body, say a fingernail or some hair, could be used to work that person's will even after being removed from the body. Think about that next time you cut off your long and scraggly toenails and flush them down the toilet. In the times of superstitious primitive peoples just learning the laws of nature, those fingernails could be powerful objects that could help you work some hoodoo out in the world, if you knew how to master the forces behind them. Think forward a bit to the Biblical tale of Samson and Delilah, and the importance of Samson's long hair. Without it, he was powerless, as Delilah the temptress proved when she chopped off his locks while he was out cold—a perfect example of how a motif can pass down from one cultural point in history to another, and even into the halls of religion and even science.

These branches of magic played a large part in the stories Frazer examined, and again we are reminded that today's science was once magical fantasy. We now know our DNA can be left behind at a scene of a crime, or that our own blood can be taken out and stored offsite in case we need it during surgery later in life.

The idea of deifying or worshipping the sun, moon, trees, crops, the sex act, eggs, bunnies, corn, and other purely natural things seems so silly to us now, but to those from whom we've descended, there was a deep understanding of the importance of those very things, even if they way they expressed that importance is now considered naïve, crude, and misinformed!

With the industrial age, many societies and cultures no longer needed folklore as a way to create their own regional identities, especially the poor, who often felt invisible and ignored. Commoners, as in the lower classes, moved from place to place seeking jobs and the folk tales of their youth that were left behind as they progressed. But it never really killed folklore; it just changed it, as the populace itself changed. The core stories have held on rather well throughout the course of history, even into today's modern age of technology, proving that everyone loves a good story, especially if it holds within it some fact or truth.

An excerpt from the First Annual Report of the Council of the English Folklore Society, published in *The Folk Lore Record* in 1879, makes a great point:

> Folk-lore may be said to include all the "culture" of the people which has not been worked into the official religion and history, but which is and has always been of self growth. It represents itself in civilized history by strange and uncouth customs; super-stitious associations with animals, birds, flowers, trees and topo-graphical objects, and with the events of human life; the belief in witchcraft, fairies, and spirits; the traditional ballads and pro-verbial sayings incident to particular localities; the retention of popular names for hills, streams, caverns, springs, tumuli, foun-tains, fields, trees, etc., and all such out-of-the-way lore.

It is that "out-of-the-way" lore that still captures our imaginations today.

Fairytales

Fairytales, more than any other type of written story-telling, com-bine imaginative and fantastical elements with archetypal characters and yet also convey important messages about life, its ups and downs and ins and out, to the conscious and subconscious mind. Most fairy-tales follow the journey of a hero or heroine who is isolated from society, whether by choice or by force, and must overcome distinct challenges and struggles, even hardships beyond measure, to come out a "happily even after" winner. Fairytale characters and motifs especially relate to younger readers and to children, because many of the characters themselves are prepubescent or preadolescent.

By definition, the term *fairytale* is a short story (oral or written) filled with fantastical and even folkloric elements such as fairies, goblins, giants, dwarves, talking trees and animals, elves, and other creatures widely accepted as imaginative and enchanting. Magic plays a role in fairytales, both good magic and evil, and they may have a happy ending, such as those fairytale romances many modern-day Hollywood movies are based upon, where the prince rescues the damsel in distress and all is well. Fairies are not always required, although they often make an appearance, and the term *fairytale,* which may have originated with 17th-century French writer Marie-Catherine Le Jumel de Barneville, also known as Baroness d'Aulnoy or Countess d'Aulnoy, who called her own stories *contes de fees* (fairytales), implies more of a particular genre than exact content.

Fairytales are also one of the categories of folklore referred to as *"Märchen,"* folktales characterized by elements of magic or the supernatural, with lead characters that often are endowed with magical powers or special knowledge; variations expose the hero to supernatural beings or objects. Märchen often begin with a formula such as "once upon a time," while remaining quite vague as to when and where. The main theme is triumph over adversity for the hero/heroine, who may be beautiful or incredibly handsome, and can involve the aid of magical creatures or powers, often against a very stylized enemy such as wicked stepmothers, stupid ogres, and mean witches. More ancient tales expose the social conditions of their times, such as matriarchy, primitive birth and marriage customs, and distributions of royal wealth and power. Often the poor and lowly hero meets the princess of the king and, through luck, cleverness, or magic, wins her hand in marriage and automatically inherits the kingdom—or vice versa, as in the

Cinderella story of a poor, abused young girl who wins the heart of the prince with the help of a fairy godmother, a pumpkin coach, and a magical glass slipper.

Fairytales all over the world are identical in content, even though their country of origins may be unknown. There are two main theories as to how this may have happened. One theory points to an original story that was then spread throughout centuries to other countries and cultures as people repeated them orally when they traveled. The second theory suggests that these stories arose at generally the same time with the same content because they reflect common human experiences that cross cultural boundaries.

Two Grimm Guys

Though fairytales did originate orally, the first systematic attempt to transcribe and record them from the oral tradition was the collection *Kinder-und Hausmärchen,* or *Children's and Household Tales* (1812–15) of the Brothers Grimm, popularly known as *Grimm's Fairy Tales.* The fairytales of the Brothers Grimm, Jacob and Wilhelm, had a much darker edge to them and were often intended just as much for adult audiences as for children. Themes of sexuality, violence, and even cruelty that were a part of the Grimm tales may have served a useful

Figure 4-1: The Brothers Grimm: Jacob and Wilhelm Grimm.

psychological purpose for children and adults as a means of solving deeper, often subconscious, issues.

Some of the more popular Grimm tales included:

Hansel and Grethel (Hansel and Gretel)

Rapunzel

Snow White and Red Rose

Cinderella

Rumpelstiltskin

Tom Thumb

Mary's Child

Brementown Musicians (Town Musicians of Bremen)

The Wedding of Mrs. Fox

The Elves and the Shoemaker

Little Briar-Rose (Sleeping Beauty)

The Golden Goose

Grimm tales influenced a host of other writings and to this day are retold and reworded as television shows, fantasy/sci-fi novels, and motion pictures.

According to Dr. Marie-Louise von Franz, author of *The Interpretation of Fairy Tales,* fairytales can even include such Jungian concepts as the shadow, the anima and the animus, and the heroes and heroines, as well as other key figures, and may take on archetypal qualities that make these stores resonate with us on a deeper, subconscious level. Another concept she explores is the possibility that primitive peoples might have been projecting their own internal states into these symbolic stories, and that a Jungian approach to analyzing them reveals insights into our own psyches and the challenges that are specifically human. Fairytales, Franz suggests, speak not just to the Self, but to the Collective Self as well, and have meaning and messages for both.

Ballads, Songs, and Nursery Rhymes

Not every story had to come down to us as spoken word or written text. Sometimes, you could convey more meaning by singing your story than writing it. Ballads have a long history, dating back to the wandering minstrels, or servants of the courts, of medieval Europe in the late 14th century, and became highly popularized as a form of love story told in verse. By the late 13th century, many court minstrels had become adept at entertaining the lords and ladies of the court with song and performances. Later ballads in the 16th century sometimes took on a very vulgar tone, called "broadside ballads," and later ballads of the 18th century often involved lyrics about economic and class struggles. Ballads, like any other form of communication, provided a unique means of expressing what was on the minds of the people at the time.

Folk songs, like folklore, allowed stories to be transmitted to music or in song, and date back before the 19th century, incorporating a number of genres such as sea shanties, holiday carols, Wassail songs, traditional children's songs, ballads, and even drinking songs.

The most popular folk song of all time and the most recognized song in the English language is "Happy Birthday to You," the melody of which was written back in 1893 by two sisters, Patty and Mildred Hill, who then fashioned it as "Good Morning to All." The song was first put in print form in 1912 with the lyrics we continue to sing today.

The most popular form of folk song is the nursery rhyme, one that most of us have grown up with and continue to pass on to our own children. These silly children's songs, which were often used during games like jumping rope and dancing, sound completely fantastical and may not make any sense at all, yet even these served a purpose as reflections of historical people, times, and events.

Some nursery rhymes were even thought to be cheeky parodies of political and royal officials hidden inside their rhythmic lyrics and beats. English nursery rhymes in particular often suggested more historical origins that were instilled in the memories of those living at the time, such as "London Bridges," "London Bells," and "Oranges and Lemons," which are said to re-create the chimes of old London churches.

In 1881, Kate Greenaway published the seminal *Mother Goose* nursery rhymes, also called *The Old Nursery Rhymes,* which included some of the very first print appearances of far older nursery rhymes and is probably one of the most important books in most older generations' childhood bookshelves, introducing us to such classics as "Hickory, Dickory, Dock," "Little Miss Muffet," "Jack Sprat," "The Cat and the Fiddle," "Georgy Porgy," and "Little Bo Peep."

Some argument and debate continues over the veracity of some nursery rhymes as true events. Let's take "Three Blind Mice," for example. Could this have been alluding to 16th-century Queen (Bloody) Mary I, who enjoyed torturing and killing? The three mice may have been three noblemen who decided she was a bit crazy and were prosecuted for conspiring to take down the Bloody Queen!

How about that egghead, Humpty Dumpty, who sat on a wall, had a great fall, and couldn't be put back together again? "Humpty Dumpty" originated in printed form for the first time in 1810. At the time, a "humpty dumpty" suggested a klutz or clumsy person, and may have been referring to King Richard III of England falling off his horse. Another suggestion is that the hapless egg refers to the downfall of Cardinal Wolsey at the hand of King Henry VIII.

And what of "Ring Around the Rosie," which has been suggested as alluding to the Black Plague? So apparently, this little ditty about joining hands in a circle, sneezing one's brains out, and then falling down as ashes might have been all about people dropping dead from the Plague. Dating back to 1347, the lyrics to this particular nursery rhyme have gone under more scrutiny than any other, including a tongue-lashing by a Website called Snopes.com that claims to debunk and find the truth about anything.

"Ring-a-ring o' roses,

A pocket full of posies,

A-tishoo! A-tishoo!

We all fall down."

Snopes.com dissected the silly song, and showed that there were many variant forms and dates of the song, many of which had no references at all that might even suggest it was describing death by plague. That the written form of the song didn't appear until 1881 also made it difficult to believe that the song even began back in 1347, about the time of the plague, at all.

Interestingly, many folklore scholars think these little ditties might have been a way to get around the ban on dancing imposed by Protestants in the 19th century in Britain and North America. By creating these "ring-games" or "play parties," as they became known, children could get around the ban and dance to their content because there was no musical accompaniment to label their activities actual dancing.

Or just maybe, as with most modern song lyrics, these nursery rhymes were just words thrown together without any regard to meaning, and were purely imaginative, catchy, and fun excuses for partying under the noses of those who disapproved.

Nursery rhymes point to the difficulties of interpretation, which occur with any transmission of ideas, concepts, and stories, because unless we know the exact motive of the person or persons responsible for creating them, we can guess until the cow jumps over the moon what they were meant for and if they held any grains of historical truth whatsoever.

And there is the Big Question: No matter their format or structure, were these stories trying to tell us something, other than just purely entertain us? Were they hiding within their structure and plot and character, their drama and fantasy and humor and terror, actual scientific knowledge and historical events? And aren't we doing this *very thing* today, with our novels and movies and TV shows that depict realistic situations in fictional formats?

From *All the President's Men* to *Patton* to *Office Space,* movies tell us grand stories on a big screen, and sometimes they tell us about actual historical events, even as we chow down on the popcorn, Milk Duds, nachos, and Diet Coke. From *The West Wing* to *Mad Men* to *Breaking Bad* and *The Office,* television series present us with fictional series every week set in places or times or situations that not only really exist, but that we may be personally familiar with. Yet we call them "television shows" and disregard them as the modern folklore we are passing on to the future.

Novels like *North and South, Hawaii, 11/22/63, The Hunt for Red October,* and even *The Da Vinci Code* weave their spells on us—pure fiction yes, but with history, science, and religious truths woven into the fabric of the story. And even those highly fantastical science fiction and speculative movies and TV shows and stories, like *The X-Files, Walking Dead, Star Trek* and *Star Wars, Close Encounters of the Third Kind,* the *Twilight* series, *Lost, Fringe,* and every sci fi and fantasy novel ever written—all hold a grain of truth, whether historical or spiritual or scientific, that might even become the fact of tomorrow.

Yet we also have non-fiction books and true-to-life documentaries that depict actual, factual events and people. We have personal journals and blogs and news stories now that document our own times for us, and for those who one day might look back and wonder what we were trying to convey—what was important to us. Separating the fact from fiction is hard enough today, with so much potential for information to be spread that sounds accurate but isn't, or is based upon false witness, or downright disinformation. Even the hard news and journalism we once thought we could rely on as truth, and the scientific and academic textbooks that lay out the facts as we knew them, are open to change, adulteration, and interpretation.

We shouldn't turn away from fables and fairytales, folklore and legend, nursery rhymes or chivalrous romances, ballads or folk tales, as if they are nothing but purely imaginative fluff and the stuff of entertainment. Encoded deep within are things we need to know and to pass on when we leave this place, in the form of our own offerings on the written page.

Maybe with stories we are not always meant to understand their meaning on a conscious level, or even a personal one. Some stories will no doubt affect our hearts, our souls, and our psyches, even if we don't quite "get" their meaning. Some stories will hold incredible meaning to us as a collective, yet not so much as an individual—and vice versa, of course.

Even as we attempt to analyze to death what our ancestors meant for us to know from these methods of transmission of information, we might be forgetting that some messages were not meant for the analytical brain at all.

They were meant for the humanity in us.

Chapter 5

Archeoenigmas:
Things Out of Time and Place

*The researches of many eminent antiquarians
have already thrown much darkness on the
subject; and it is possible, if they continue their
labors, that we shall soon know nothing at all.*
—Artemus Ward

All over the world, enigmatic objects exist that seem out of place, even out of time, as if they were placed there by unseen means, and not at all an organic outgrowth of their environment. All over the world, there are edifices that look similar, have the same shapes, and share the same structure, as if the same designer were responsible for them all.

"Archeoenigmas" are archaeological objects and structures that are of a mysterious nature or origin. They are enigmas that we have yet to fully understand, or explain by simple means. Often, otherworldly explanations are attached to such objects and structures, as if we have been given gifts from other civilizations from other worlds that have come here, leaving behind mysteries we have yet to unravel.

Why do similar images appear on pyramids in Bolivia as on steles in Central America and the edifices of Egypt? What does it tell us about our past when the same strange entities and objects show up again and again, pointing to a history hidden in symbolism? Why are stone carvings on a pot in ancient Greece exactly like those found in ancient China?

Some people believe that everything we think we know about history is wrong, and that the traditional dogma regarding antiquity is but one tiny piece of a much larger puzzle. Our written history was forged from verbal stories and legends passed down from generation to generation, which begs the question: What if there were bits and pieces that were accidentally—or purposely—left out?

American naturalist Ivan T. Sanderson coined the term *OOPart* to describe objects that seemingly defy conventional historical chronology. These objects and articles pose a mystery—and are of great interest and importance as they challenge everything that we think we know.

According to conventional history, human beings were not present on earth 65 million years ago, yet how can we explain semi-ovoid shaped metallic tubes that have been dug out of 65-million-year-old Cretaceous chalk in France?

Back in 1912, employees at an electric plant discovered a large chunk of coal, which, when broken open, revealed an iron pot. Nails have been found deeply embedded within chunks of sandstone rock dating back to the Mesozoic Era. Beyond these, there are many, many more examples of such anomalous objects that seemingly defy traditional explanations.

What could these finding possibly mean? Well, there are a number of possibilities:

1. Our actual history dates back much, much further than recorded reports would allow.

2. There is the possibility that other intelligent beings or civilizations existed on earth before our recorded history.

3. Perhaps our dating methods are wholly incorrect, and stone, coal, and fossils may form much more rapidly than we have estimated.

In this chapter, we will focus on several of the more popular archeoenigmas and OOPart's that have been discovered throughout the world. Though fascinating in their own right, these findings should prompt the reexamination of the true history of human life on earth.

Baghdad Battery

In 1936, while workers were excavating the ruins of a 2,000-year-old ancient village near Baghdad, a mysterious small clay vase was discovered. This bright yellow clay vase contained a cylinder of copper sheet 5 inch by 1.5 inches. The edge of the copper cylinder appeared to have been soldered with a 60–40 lead-tin alloy, which is quite comparable to modern solder. The bottom of the cylinder was capped with a crimped copper disk and sealed with asphalt or bitumen. On the top of the cylinder, another layer of asphalt was utilized to seal the top, and also to hold an iron rod suspended in the center of the copper cylinder. The rod showed indications of having been corroded with an acidic substance.

After studying the enigmatic object, German archaeologist Willhem Konig came to the stunning conclusion that this seemingly innocuous clay pot was actually an ancient electric battery! But how could this be? According to our accepted history, the viable use of electricity for technological means was not discovered until 1831 when English scientist Michael Faraday created the first electric dynamo—a crude predecessor to today's modern power generators.

In 1940, an engineer named Willard F.M. Gray, who worked for the General Electric High Voltage Laboratory in Pittsfield, Massachusetts, read of Konig's theory and developed a replica of the battery. Using a copper sulfate solution, it generated about .5 volts of electricity!

In the 1970s, German Egyptologist Arne Eggebrecht also built a replica of the Baghdad battery and filled it with freshly pressed grape juice (which he speculated would have been the same substance that the ancient Egyptians might have used), and it generated 0.87 volts. Eggebrecht's model produced enough electricity that he was able to electroplate a silver statue with gold!

Since then, hundreds of individuals throughout the world have reproduced the Baghdad battery with stunning success. These experiments have all served to prove that electric battery technology was created and used nearly 1,800 years before the modern invention by Alessandro Volta in late 1799.

What could these primitive batteries have been used for? Beyond electroplating metals, some researchers have theorized that they may have been used for medicinal purposes or even as power sources for other advanced technological devices that have yet to be discovered (or perhaps rediscovered!).

Antikythera Mechanism

Sponge divers working off the isle of Antikythera discovered a very unique and interesting find in 1901. The divers found the remains of a remarkably complex clocklike mechanism. The technical complexity and engineering of the device is incredible—especially for a device that is believed to be more than 2,000 years old! After its discovery, the device sat in a museum for more than 50 years before historians began to take a serious interest in investigating its provenance and possible use.

Known as the Antikythera mechanism, it has been referred to as an intricate "clockwork computer." This small bronze device was built sometime between 150 BC and 100 BC, and is unique in that it preceded any machine or device of comparable complexity by more than a millennium.

Consisting of a small box with dials on the outside and an extremely complex assembly of gear wheels mounted within, the Antikythera mechanism resembles a finely made 18th- or 19th-century Swiss clock. External hinged doors appeared to have been placed to protect the dials, and on all available surfaces of the box, doors, and dials, were long Greek inscriptions describing the operation and construction of the device. Despite the harsh salt water conditions, at least 20 wheel gears have been preserved including an incredibly intricate assembly of gears that were mounted eccentrically on a turntable and likely functions as a type of epicyclic or differential gear system. According to the Atlas Obscura (*atlasobscura.com*), the Antikythera mechanism is

> [r]egarded as the first known analog computer, the mechanism can make precise calculations based on astronomical and mathematical principles developed by the ancient Greeks. Although its builder's identity and what it was doing aboard a ship remain mysteries, scientists have worked for a century to piece together the mechanism's history.

Somewhat surprisingly, most consider it unlikely that the Antikythera mechanism was a navigational tool. The harsh environment at sea would have presented a danger to the instrument's delicate gears, and features such as eclipse predictions are unnecessary for navigation. The mechanism's small size, however, does suggest that it was designed with portability in mind. According to some researchers, a more plausible story is that the mechanism was used to teach astronomy to those with little knowledge of the subject.

To use the instrument, you would simply enter a date using a crank, and, when the gears stopped spinning, a wealth of information appear at your fingertips: the positions of the Sun, Moon, planets, and stars, the lunar phase, the dates of upcoming solar eclipses, the speed of the Moon through the sky, and even the dates of the Olympic games. Perhaps most impressively, the mechanism's calendar dial could compensate for the extra quarter-day in the astronomical year by turning the scale back one day every four years. The Julian calendar, which was the first in the region to include leap years, was not introduced until decades after the instrument was built.

Historically, nothing of this complexity has been discovered elsewhere, and nothing even remotely comparable is known to exist in any of the scientific texts or literary references from the period. In fact, from what we do know about the technology and science of the Hellenistic period, a device such as this should not even exist! Even the most complex mechanical devices from the period contained only simple gearing systems.

This intriguing device is currently housed in the Bronze Collection of the National Archaeological Museum of Athens. A replica of the mechanism is also located at the American Computer Museum in Bozeman, Montana.

Dendera Light Bulb

Deep beneath the Temple of Hathor at Dendera there is a stone relief that seemingly depicts a "bulb like" object, which some proponents believe is an ancient light bulb! Some ancient Egyptologists believe that the technology depicted appears to be similar to a Crookes Tube, which was an early form of light bulb. Within the bulb icon, there is a snake that forms a wavy line from a lotus flower (the socket of the bulb). Connected to this is a length or wire of cable that terminates in a small box. Next to the bulb is a two-armed djed pillar, which appears to be connected to the snake, as well as a small baboon holding two knives. The discovery of this enigmatic icon has been a source of significant controversy as it represents a significant departure from traditional Egyptian history.

Among the researchers who share this view is famed Swiss archaeologist Erich von Däniken. Von Däniken is a best-selling author best known for his often-controversial theories regarding "Ancient Astronauts" and the extraterrestrial influence on early human cultures and civilizations. According to von Däniken, the presence of electrically powered light sources might help to explain the notable absence of black soot and carbon deposits in temples and tombs. In his acclaimed book *The Eyes of the Sphinx,* von Däniken theorizes that the snake might represent a filament, the djed pillar was an insulator, and the tube itself was actually an ancient electric light bulb! According to von Däniken, the baboon was a warning sign and signified that the device was dangerous if used incorrectly.

Although most components of the Dendera Light Bulb certainly could correspond with modern electrical light bulb specifications, several overarching questions remain: How could such a supposedly primitive society have acquired the knowledge and tools to develop such an advanced technology? Secondly, even if the ancient Egyptians had developed a light bulb, how was it powered? Was a device similar to the Baghdad battery employed? Why have we not discovered any surviving "light bulbs"?

Saqqara Bird

In a tomb dated 200 BCE, deep below the sands of Saqqara, Egypt, an unusual artifact was recovered in 1898. The artifact is made of well-preserved sycamore wood that was thought to originate from the tomb's epoch. Egyptian artifacts are recovered fairly often, so what makes this one unique? Well, this particular object is shaped like a modern-day airplane or glider! Due to its similar characteristics, it has been named the Saqqara Bird or Saqqara Glider. The object is approximately 5.6 inches in length, and has an overall wingspan of 7.2 inches. The artifact even has a tail section that mirrors a modern aircraft!

When it was originally discovered, the object was cataloged as a model of a bird and was stored, gathering dust, in the basement of the museum of Cairo until 1969, when it was "rediscovered" by Dr. Khalil Messiha, an Egyptologist and model plane enthusiast. Dr. Messiha immediately noticed that the artifact did not resemble any known bird species; however, it had definite similarity to an airplane! Since then, several artifacts similar to the Saqqara Bird have been recovered from various other tombs throughout Egypt.

Looking at the artifact, it certainly does appear "plane-like," as the tail is vertical like an airplane, not horizontal like a bird would be. Many individuals have built balsa wood replicas, and they have success-fully flown when thrown by hand.

Though mainstream Egyptologists believe that the Saqqara Glider may actually be a type of ceremonial object, or even a toy, several alter-native theories suggest that it was developed as a model of an actual plane or glider that was either built, or witnessed, by the Egyptians. Intriguingly, bird models that the Egyptians typically built had legs, the Saqqara Bird does not. In addition, other models have painted feath-ers; again, this one does not.

One final interesting tidbit about the Saqqara Bird: Inscribed on the side of model are hieroglyphics that say "the Gift of Amon." In ancient Egypt, Amon was known to be the God of wind and air, and the phrase "I want to fly" was allegedly found on a papyrus scroll that was discovered alongside the artifact.

Coso Artifact

From ancient Egypt, we move to the United States. In 1961, three friends were prospecting for geodes to sell in their rock shop near the small town of Olanche, California. Wallace Lane, Virginia Maxey, and Mike Mikesell had been digging for some time when they came across a specimen that was quite unusual. This particular geode appeared to be encrusted with fossilized shell fragments. In addition, they noticed two non-magnetic metallic objects protruding from the crest. Amazingly, these resembled a nail and a washer!

The next day, while at the store, Mike Mikesell attempted to cut the specimen in half. During the process, Mikesell claims to have ruined a nearly new diamond saw blade. Inside, he discovered a perfectly circular section of extremely hard, dense white material that appeared to be ceramic or porcelain. In the center of the ceramic substrate, there was a 2-millmeter shaft of shiny material that responded to a magnet. Mikesell immediately recognized the object as a modern-era spark plug!

Virginia Maxey claims to have taken the unusual object to a geologist who dated the artifact to be approximately 500,000 years old. To date, we do not know the geologist's name or what methods were used to date the object. For an object of this potential significance, it seems highly suspect that the geologist has never been identified, nor have his findings been published in any known trade journal. Furthermore, at the time the geologist has supposedly dated the Coso Artifact as being approximately 500,000 years old, there was no known method (such as the use of guide fossils) by which either the artifact or the concretions could have been accurately dated.

From "The Coso Artifact: Mystery From the Depths of Time?" by Pierre Stromberg and Paul Heinrich:

> To help us to learn more about spark-plug technology of a century ago, we enlisted the help of the Spark Plug Collectors of America (SPCA). We sent letters to four different spark plug collectors describing the Coso Artifact, including Calais's X-rays of the object in question. We expected the SPCA to provide some vague hints or no information at all about the artifact. The actual answers were stunning.

On September 9, 1999, Chad Windham, president of the SPCA, called Pierre Stromberg. Windham initially suspected that Stromberg was a fellow spark plug collector, writing incognito, with the motive of hoaxing him. His fears were compounded by the fact that there is an actual line of spark plugs named "Stromberg." Though Stromberg repeatedly assured Windham that his intentions were purely for research, he was puzzled why Windham was so suspicious and asked him to explain. Windham replied that it was so obvious to him that the artifact was a contemporary spark plug, the letter had to be a hoax. "I knew what it was the moment I saw the X-rays," Windham wrote.

Stromberg asked Windham if he could identify the particular make of the spark plug. Windham replied he was certain that it was a 1920s-era Champion spark plug. Later, Windham sent two identical spark plugs for comparison. Ten days after Windham's telephone call, Bill Bond, founder of the SPCA and curator of a private museum of spark plugs containing more than 2,000 specimens, called Stromberg. Bond said he thought he knew the identity of the Coso Artifact: "a 1920s Champion spark plug." Spark plug collectors Mike Healy and Jeff Bartheld (vice president of the SPCA) also concurred with Bond's and Windham's assessment about the spark plug. To date, there has been no dissent among the spark plug collectors as to the identity of the Coso Artifact.

Researchers today are divided regarding their beliefs as to the true origin of the Coso Artifact. It is likely that this enigmatic object is likely to remain controversial for the foreseeable future.

The Georgia Guidestones

Situated on a hilltop field 8 miles outside of the town of Elberton, Georgia, the Georgia Guidestones stand proudly as a testament to modern engineering and machinations. Modern? Yes, the construction of the Georgia Guidestones is well known. However, the details become murky beyond that.

Sometimes referred to as the "American Stonehenge," the Georgia Guidestones are a megalithic monument that was erected in 1980 by the Elberton Granite Finishing Company. The stones are engraved in eight different languages (English, Spanish, Swahili, Hindi, Hebrew, Arabic, Chinese, and Russian) and relay 10 "commandments" for "an Age of Reason." The stones were situated in a manner in which the winter and summer solstices could be delineated. The rocks are absolutely massive—and the quarrying, transportation, and erection are considered an amazing engineering feat even by today's standards!

Figure 5-1: The Georgia Guidestones. Image courtesy of Larry Flaxman.

Each rock is 16 feet tall, with four of the blocks weighing more than 20 tons each. Together, they form the support for a 25,000-pound capstone. On each of the stones, the following sayings are inscribed:

1. Maintain humanity under 500,000,000 in perpetual balance with nature.

2. Guide reproduction wisely—improving fitness and diversity.

3. Unite humanity with a living new language.

4. Rule passion—faith—tradition—and all things with tempered reason.

5. Protect people and nations with fair laws and just courts.

6. Let all nations rule internally resolving external disputes in a world court.

7. Avoid petty laws and useless officials.

8. Balance personal rights with social duties.

9. Prize truth—beauty—love—seeking harmony with the infinite.

10. Be not a cancer on the earth—Leave room for nature—Leave room for nature.

Like most things "unknown," the Georgia Guidestones have attracted many conspiratorial theories regarding its meaning. Theories abound regarding the true meaning behind the stones—with some believing that they have a satanic or Luciferian origin. Others believe that the Guidestones are actually an iconic representation of the New World Order (NWO)—and exemplify the beliefs that the secret "shadow government" supposedly espouses.

In 2009, *Wired* magazine ran a story on the Guidestones and provided a significant amount of background information regarding the origin of these mysterious stones. However, there are still many, many unexplained aspects of the story. According to the story, a man named Robert C. Christian showed up in Elberton County one day in June

1979, claiming to represent "a small group of loyal Americans" who had been planning the installation of an unusually large and complex stone monument. Christian had chosen Elberton—the granite capital of the world—because its quarries were said to produce the finest stone on the planet.

Joe Fendley, Elberton Granite's president, was intrigued by the description Christian gave of the monument he had in mind, which would include stones larger than any that had been quarried in the county, and stones that were to be cut, finished, and assembled into some kind of enormous "astronomical instrument."

Christian explained to Fendley that the structure would serve several purposes—as a compass, calendar, and clock—and would need to be engraved with a set of guides written in eight of the world's major languages. Christian insisted it had to be capable of withstanding catastrophes and natural disasters, so that the shattered remnants of humanity would be able to use those guides to reestablish a better civilization than the one that was about to destroy itself.

Construction of the Guidestones got under way later that summer. Hundreds of photographs were taken to document the progress of the work. Jackhammers were used to gouge 114 feet into the rock at Pyramid Quarry, searching for hunks of granite big enough to yield the final stones. Fendley and his crew held their breath when the first 28-ton slab was lifted to the surface, wondering if their derricks would buckle under the weight. A special burner (essentially a narrowly focused rocket motor used to cut and finish large blocks of granite) was trucked to Elberton to clean and size the stones, and a pair of master stonecutters was hired to smooth them.

Then began the search for a suitable site for the Guidestones in Elberton County: a flat-topped hill rising above the pastures of the Double 7 Farms, with vistas in all directions. For $5,000, owner Wayne Mullinex signed over a 5-acre plot. In addition to the payment,

Christian granted lifetime cattle-grazing rights to Mullinex and his children, and Mullinex's construction company got to lay the foundation for the Guidestones.

With the purchase of the land, the Guidestones' future was set.

Apparently, a carefully cut slot in the Guidestones' center column frames the sunrise on solstices and equinoxes. The astrological specifications for the Guidestones were so complex that Fendley had to retain the services of an astronomer from the University of Georgia to help implement the design. The four outer stones were to be oriented based on the limits of the sun's yearly migration. The center column needed two precisely calibrated features: a hole through which the North Star would be visible at all times, and a slot that was to align with the position of the rising sun during the solstices and equinoxes. The principal component of the capstone was a 7/8-inch aperture through which a beam of sunlight would pass at noon each day, shining on the center stone to indicate the day of the year. Was this another Stonehenge? Was that what Christian had intended to build, an American version of that amazing British monument?

The main feature of the monument, though, would be the 10 dictates carved into both faces of the outer stones, in eight languages: English, Spanish, Russian, Chinese, Arabic, Hebrew, Hindi, and Swahili. A mission statement of sorts (LET THESE BE GUIDESTONES TO AN AGE OF REASON) was also to be engraved on the sides of the capstone in Egyptian hieroglyphics, classical Greek, Sanskrit, and Babylonian cuneiform. The United Nations provided some of the translations (including those for the dead languages), which were stenciled onto the stones and etched with a sandblaster.

The monument ignited controversy before it was even finished. The first rumor began among members of the Elberton Granite Association, jealous of the attention being showered on one of their own: Fendley was behind the whole thing, they said, aided by his friend Martin, the banker. The gossip became so poisonous that the two men agreed to take a lie detector test at the Elberton Civic Center. The scandal withered when *The Elberton Star* reported that they had both passed convincingly, but the publicity brought a new wave of complaints. As word of what was being inscribed spread, Martin recalls, even people he considered friends asked him why he was doing the devil's work. According to the article in *Wired,* a local minister, James Travenstead, predicted that "occult groups" would flock to the Guidestones, warning that "someday a sacrifice will take place here." Those inclined to agree were hardly discouraged by Charlie Clamp, the sandblaster charged with carving each of the 4,000-plus characters on the stones: During the hundreds of hours he spent etching the guides, Clamp said, he had been constantly distracted by strange music and disjointed voices.

Recently, while in Georgia, I (Larry) spent some time at the Georgia Guidestones. I wanted to see for myself why these megalithic stones seemed to attract such a controversial following. I was given rare, unprecedented access to information from several key members of the community who had information regarding the design and construction of the monument. Amazingly, I was even able to interview one of the central individuals (and who was alleged to be a part of the conspiracy himself!). According to this individual, the Guidestones was designed to be nothing more than an elaborate "advertising" program intended to boost the local marble and stonework trade.

There are many theories regarding this mysterious edifice, and I came away from the experience with more questions than answers. Although I certainly have my own ideas regarding the identity of the mysterious "R.C. Christian" and his motivations behind building the Georgia Guidestones, this structure shrouded in secrecy and mystery will likely remain an enigmatic part of Georgia history.

Kensington Runestone

Throughout the Unites States, several runestones have been discovered that seem to defy traditional world and archeological history. There is considerable controversy regarding the two most popular: the Kensington Runestone in Minnesota and the Heavener Runestone in Oklahoma. Many believe that these stones have been created in modern times as a hoax to claim that Scandinavian explorers reached the middle of North America sometime during the 14th century. Of course, this would significantly impact our mainstream, accepted account of history!

The 36x16x6-inch, 200-pound Kensington Runestone, containing runic writing along the face and one side, was discovered in 1898 in the rural township of Solem, Douglas County, Minnesota. The runestone was named after the closest settlement, Kensington, and the community of Kensington is steadfast in its assertion that that the glyph is legitimate. Nearly all experts in Scandanavian linguistics who have analyzed the stone believe it to be a cleverly concocted hoax.

According to the legend, the stone was discovered by a Minnesota farmer named Olaf Ohman in November 1889 while he was digging up a poplar tree stump situated on the southern slope of a 50-foot-high knoll. Ohman stated that the stone was buried face down approximately 6 inches below the surface of the soil, and numerous tree roots were wrapped around it. Years after unearthing it, the stone was sent to the University of Minnesota, then to the University of Chicago, where it was analyzed by runic scholars, who allegedly interpreted the inscriptions to be a detailed historical account of Norse explorers during the 14th century. Since the initial analysis, other authorities have examined the stone and have claimed it to be a forgery; however, many also assert its authenticity.

Historically, we do know that King Magnus of Sweden sent an exploratory party to Greenland in 1355, and these brave voyagers never returned. Some individuals believe that these men may have been from that expedition. The stone itself has little clues as to its true origin.

The transliteration of the stones text is generally accepted to be: "Eight Goths and 22 Norwegians on a journey of exploration from Vinland very far west. We had camp by 2 rocky islands one day's journey north from this stone. We were out fishing one day. After we came home we found 10 men red with blood and dead. AVM [Ave Maria] save us from evil."

Along the edge of the stone, the inscription says: "Have 10 men by the sea to look after our ships 14 days' journey from this island. Year 1362."

In a 2000 conference attended by archaeologists from 20 states and three Canadian provinces, a Minnesota geologist working in tandem with a Wisconsin chemist presented what they believe is indisputable, compelling evidence that the runestone inscription is "real" and legitimately antique, probably from the 1300s.

To date, there has been no absolute scientific proof provided either for or against the authenticity of the stone that would definitively put to rest the mystery of the Kensington Runestone.

Object of Aiud

In 1973, near the Romanian city of Aiud, a group of construction workers were digging along the banks of the Mures River when they discovered three unusual objects buried in a sand trench 33 feet deep. Two of the objects recovered were Mastodon bones dating from between the Miocene and Pleistocene periods. The third object was an unusual "hammer"-shaped block. This wedge-shaped block weighed approximately 5 pounds and contained several odd features. Due to the unusual nature of the find, the objects were sent to researchers in the city of Cluj Napoca. There, scientists discovered that the block was actually metal and contained two cylindrical holes of different sizes that appeared to have been made in such a way that the hole with the smaller diameter perpendicularly penetrated the base of the other cylindrical hole. The larger hole was oval shaped, and it appeared that it might have been attached to a shaft. The object had numerous surface marks that indicated repeated strong strikes along the face. All of the details suggest that the object might have been a part of a larger functional assembly and was lost in the riverbank due to unknown reasons.

ICPMNN (The Magurele Research Institute) conducted a metallurgical analysis of the object and determined that the composition of the object was very unusual—and very complex. According to their assay, the Object of Aiud was composed of 12 different elements, and 89 percent of the alloy was aluminum. The other components were found to be: silicon—2.84 percent, zinc—0.81 percent, lead—0.41 percent, tin—0.33 percent, zirconium—0.2 percent, cadmium—0.0024 percent, cobalt—0.0023 percent, bismuth—0.0003 percent, and silver—0.0002 percent, along with minute traces of gallium.

So, the object was basically composed of aluminum. However, the age of the object was established to be 250,000 years old! This presents a slight problem as aluminum was not discovered until 1825, cadmium in 1817, nickel in 1751, bismuth in 1753, and cobalt in 1735.

The Baigong Pipes

Are they pipes? Are they trees? Are they proof of aliens? There are allegendly hundreds of rustic pipes made of iron running deep into Mount Baigong in rural China, with other such pipes running into the lake bottom nearby and along the lake shoreline. These pipes appear to be finely and cleanly cut and have been dated back to more than 5,000 years ago, according to some archeologists. There is little information on these mysterious pipes that are not where they should be, most of it coming from a June 19, 2002, article from *Xinhuanet* titled "Chinese Scientists to Head for Suspected ET Relics." The article claims that the mysterious site near Delingha City in the depths of the Qaidam Basin is known by local people as "the ET relics structure," which looks like a pyramid and is between 50 to 60 meters high. One of the three caves in the area, all of which have triangular openings, sports a half-pipe inside of about 40 centimeters diameter, and above the cave are about a dozen pipes of various diameters which run into the mountain.

According to Qin Jianwen, head of the publicity department of the Delingha government, the reddish brown pipe scraps were once taken to a local smeltery for analysis and were shown to contain 30 percent ferric oxide and a large amount of silicon dioxide and calcium oxide. Eight percent of the content could not be identified. "The large content of silicon dioxide and calcium oxide is a result of long interaction between iron and sandstone, which means the pipes must be very old," said Liu Shaolin, the engineer who did the analysis.

"This result has made the site even more mysterious," Qin said. "Nature is harsh here. There are no residents let alone modern industry in the area, only a few migrant herdsmen to the north of the mountain."

Because of the high altitude the suggestion arose among locals that the area might have been an extraterrestrial hangout, and the pipes are somehow proof of that claim. But researchers and skeptics point out that these "pipes" may just be fossilized casts of trees, washed into the Qaidam basin as flood debris and subsequently incorporated into sandstone, especially because original organic material was found in the "pipes" as well as fossilized tree rings. Some researchers think they might be made of bamboo, which would explain their long, straight pipe-like appearance, but wouldn't explain the tree rings.

The mystery persists, though, perhaps more due to local legend than any actual alien or mysterious origin.

Pyramid Power

Throughout the world, there are literally thousands of pyramid-shaped structures built. But why? Any more importantly, how was the information communicated among disparate cultures? Although the Great Pyramid of Giza is the most famous pyramid, there are actually eight others of various sizes in Giza alone! Amazingly, these complex-shaped structures have been discovered all over Egypt—in locations such as Saqqara, Medium, El-Lahun, Hawara, and Abu Rawash.

In the United States there are a few as well. Although most North American pyramids are constructed of dirt and are generally referred to as "mounds," the similarity is nevertheless obvious. Munks Mount at Cohokia (near Collinsville, Illinois), the Etowah Mounds (Cartersville, Georgia), and the Miamisburg "serpent" Mound (Ohio) all bear striking similarities with other pyramidal structures found throughout the world.

In Central America and South America, hundreds of pyramid structures have been discovered, including many step pyramids. Scientists believe that these Mayan mysteries have taken stylistic cues from the ancient Babylonians such as the large stepped levels with center rising staircases. Built in 683 AD for Lord Pacal, the Pyramid of Inscription is probably the most well known of the Central American Pyramids. Other noted Central American pyramids are the Pyramid of Kukulkan, as well as the Pyramid of The Sun and the Pyramid of the Moon, which are the largest of approximately 600 different structures found on the site. In the Lima region of Peru are the Caral Pyramids, of which the Huaca Larga is believed to be the largest pyramid found in South America.

Believe it or not, there are several pyramids that have been found in Greece as well. Although not well known, 16 known Greek pyramids have been discovered. Most of these pyramids appear to be monumental edifices to soldiers who perished during combat. Fourteen of the 16 pyramids are in ruins, 1lthough two fully intact ones have been discovered in Helleniko and Ligourio.

Figure 5-2:
Image courtesy of
thomaswanhoff

Figure 5-3: Image
courtesy of Alex
Covarrubias.

Two very similar step pyramids, found across the globe from one another. The first (figure 5-2) is the Koh Ker, in Cambodia. The second (figure 5-3) is El Castillo, at Chichen-Itza, Mexico.

In Europe, one controversial pyramid—the Bosnian Pyramid—has come under intense scrutiny and debate from scientists and historians, and has been declared a cruel hoax, although evidence and opinions differ as to its legitimacy. Many of the other pyramids that have been discovered in Europe are believed to have been influenced by the Christian religion, although, again, little written evidence has been found to support claims for or against extra cultural influence.

Was it just a love for pyramid-shaped objects inherent in our human nature that gave rise to the prevalence of such edifices across the globe, or a general understanding of the power of the shape itself as a symbol of energy going from the ground up to a pinpoint at the top, then shooting out into the cosmos—or vice versa?

Some archeologists argue that no mysterious explanation is needed, as cultures had similar patterns of evolution and progression, including that of ideas and innovations. Yet there are those who argue that the only way information could jump across oceans and vast bodies of land would be at the hands of outside influences—even aliens.

Perhaps the true explanations are known only to a select few who are sworn to secrecy....

Chapter 6

Hidden Wisdom, Secret Truths

There are no secrets that time does not reveal.
            —Jean Racine

Some people think that the truth can be hidden with a little cover-up and decoration. But as time goes by, what is true is revealed, and what is fake fades away.

            —Ismail Haniyeh

There was a time—in fact, many times—throughout history when certain truths had to be hidden from the authority figures, whether religious or political, in power. Truth, scientific knowledge, spiritual wisdom—all were considered dangerous to those who made the rules and kept control of the populace, whether because that truth and knowledge would cut the rulers out of power, or they would simply overturn society if they were to become visible. So, they were hidden, in the form of objects and symbols, often in the hands of those who either individually or collectively made the choice to risk their own lives to carry that knowledge forward so that it would not be lost.

Lone occultists, secret societies, diviners, and mystics all played a role in the encoding and transmission of certain truths down through history, and we can only imagine how much of that truth was lost when they were burned at the stake, slaughtered, imprisoned, and tortured, their objects and writings and teachings burned along with them.

Secrets and Societies

Hidden information usually took on the form of symbols that were only to be understood either to the chosen few, or those enlightened enough to understand their intentions. Via art and even architecture, even something like playing cards, someone could encode visuals that were meant to look like mere decorative touches, yet held secrets—sometimes powerful secrets—for the discerning eye.

Through much of the Middle Ages, or medieval times, between the fifth and 15th centuries AD, ancient civilization went screaming and kicking into a more modern period of the Late Middle Ages. But first humanity had to survive the "Dark Ages" of intellectual degradation, religious fanaticism, and cultural depression, before we collectively entered the "light" of the Italian Renaissance period in the 14th century. During these darker times, invasions and inquisitions were the order of the day, often in the name of religious fervor and judgmental righteousness. The Islamic Empire was spreading in North Africa by the seventh century, and in the West, Christianity expanded its grasp into Western Europe.

One kingdom was overtaken by another, one empire unseated another, one religion drove out another, and any teachings, wisdom, or knowledge that went against the authority of the day was considered grounds for death, even torture. Whereas the High Middle Age period had its crusades (religious wars that were conducted by European Catholics against pagan holdouts, heretics, and Muslims to attempt to control them, wipe them out entirely, or absorb them into Catholicism), the earlier 12th–14th centuries had the Inquisition. The goal of the Roman Catholic Inquisition was to quell religious sectarianism and wipe out heretics, especially those of a Cathar or Waldesian persuasion.

The Inquisition that began early on in the 12th century was later expanded to other countries, and other enemies fell within the targets of these organized "witch hunts," including the Knights Templar, Hindus, and Muslims, and, in the case of the later Portuguese Inquisition, the Sephardic Jews, who were captured and forced to convert to Christianity, all the way up to the actual witch burnings of the 18th century in Europe and the Unites States, as well as Asia and Africa.

These religious holy wars intended to not only wipe out any heresy, but also make a direct warning to those who spread the knowledge of occult or esoteric concepts, especially any that went against Catholic teachings, and questioned the power and authority of the Church. It was indeed a "dark age" for ideas, open thought and debate, religious freedom, freedom of expression, and the desire to be enlightened or pursue esoteric knowledge without the need of a Church middleman to assist you on the journey.

Esotericism is simply the practice of esoteric beliefs, often in a small and secret group of special initiates devoted to preserving and passing on those beliefs. The word comes from the Greek *esoterikos,* which means within, referring to a body of inner knowledge. Like esoteric knowledge, the occult, taken from the Latin *occultus,* meaning hidden and secret, is a body of knowledge only accessible to the adept or initiated, usually of a magical and mystical bent, but often including a real interest in science, such as the teachings of alchemy.

Occult and esoteric teachings can encompass anything from astrology, alchemy, theosophy, spiritualism, Rosicrucianism, Hermetica, Kabbalah, Gnosticism, Satanism, Wicca, Thelema, and Freemasonry, to name a few philosophies and mystical movements under the banner of hidden and secret wisdom groups. Because many of these teachings went against the authoritative and religious norms of the times, they were kept as secret as possible, despite the fact that many members might also hold high religious and political positions or positions of power in society.

Really, all these beliefs were trying to do was go beyond the rigorous boundaries of both scientific knowledge and religious acceptance, with the two at either end of a yardstick that, in the center, held more spiritual, arcane truths. Mainstream religion might have an esoteric or mystic arm, such as Christian Mystics and Sufism, but they were allowed to operate in a bit more freedom than some of the edgier occult organizations. There were common threads in most esoteric traditions, such as a belief in a life force; a belief in the "as above, so below" correspondence of cosmic and natural laws; the use of mediators such as divination tools, angels, spirit guides, adepts, and rituals to achieve the direct experience of spiritual truths; and the personal transformation of enlightenment and truth.

Again, much of this activity had to be done on the "down low" to avoid the wrath of the powerful institutions that survived by control and authority, so the idea of anyone achieving spiritual enlightenment or attaining spiritual truth was in direct conflict with the need to keep the people under the proverbial thumb. The Catholic Church, most notably, had no use for anyone who didn't see it and its practitioners as the only way to truth, and heretics and blasphemers experienced all sorts of wonderful tortures at the hands of those who refused to cut out the mystical middleman between the divine force and us.

The Cathar Story

One perfect example of an early "secret society," a group designed to carry on knowledge and secrets under the radar of watchful eyes, that operated under such spiritually and intellectually suffocating conditions was the Cathars. Also called the Albigensians, the Cathars were members of a religious sect in Europe, mainly in southern France and Italy, in the 12th and 13th centuries. They were considered heretical by the Catholic Church at the time, and paid the price by being slaughtered into non-existence at the hands of the Albigensian Crusade ordered by

Pope Innocent III beginning in 1209 AD. The Cathars were dualists, and because they associated materialism with evil, they led simple, aesthetic lives. But that's not what pissed off the Church. Cathars denied the material body of Jesus and instead viewed him as a spiritual entity in a spirit body. They believed that good was of the spirit and heavenly, and evil was of man and the material world. Thus they despised the Catholic Church's lavish architecture and wealth as evil. They also refused to acknowledge the pope as an authority figure and practiced a form of non-resistance similar to Buddhism.

In other words, the Cathars were a peaceful people. They referred to themselves as "The Pure Ones," feeling their own belief system to be far more pure than the money, power, and greed of the Catholic Church. Their priests were called "perfecti" and gave up all worldly possessions in a quest for purity, and all Cathars lived as they believed Jesus would have lived and were treated as equals, including women, which angered the Catholic Church to no end. They were also adept at the use of occult symbolism and may have revered Mary Magdalene as a partner to Jesus, suggested as well by the Nag Hammadi texts found in Egypt in 1945, in which the Gospel of Phillip mentions Jesus proclaiming the mystery of marriage as "great" when asked about his relationship with the Magdalene. This also aligns with the concept of "Pure Ones" having an origin in their belief in the Goddess/Creator Mother Mari (some believe a prototype of Eve), according to William Henry in *Secrets of the Cathars: Why the Dark Age Church Was Out to Destroy Them.* Henry suggests that the Cathars may have possessed a divinely written *Book of Love,* the handiwork of Jesus himself who gave it to John the Divine and was later adopted by the Knights Templar as well (who, by the way, were the victims of another Catholic Crusade). The Holy Grail, to the Cathars, was not a cup, but a process by which our own body could be made into a spiritual and worthy vehicle for the light of love, or the Holy Spirit. According to Henry:

The existence of this lost, or hidden, gospel was revealed when the Catholic Church subjected the Cathars and Templar (in 1308) to torture. Its contents were a secret skill (symbolized by a Templar skull) said to grant one the ability to control the forces of nature and to transform ordinary human blood into that of the wise, holy and pure blood of life of the immortal Illi or Illuminati. It is equated with the Holy Grail.

(Note the name Illuminati. More on that and the Templar connection in a bit.)

Many Cathars, before the Crusade, settled in the Languedoc region west of Marseilles in southern France, where it soon became the majority religion in the area, with many adherents that included some defectors from the Church itself, and it is there that so many traces of Magdalenian worship still exist, and there are whispers from the past to the present of this being the potential burial place of Christ himself. Cathar belief also suggested that Mary and Jesus had offspring.

So to make a very long story short, these Cathars were slaughtered by the Catholic Crusaders over a period of two generations, and the few who survived scattered across the region and laid low. But the big mystery that remains to this day surrounds a "Cathar treasure" that was somehow smuggled out of the fortress at Montsegur right before it was seized and the slaughter began, a treasure that might be untold amounts of silver and gold, the Holy Grail itself, the blood of Mary Magdalene, who had arrived in southern France earlier, the burial place of Christ, and, as many believe, a written bloodline of Christ and his offspring with the Magdalene. In any regards, some believe the treasure is still in the region, possibly buried deep below a place called Rennes-le-Chateau.

Rennes-le-Chateau

At the top of a hill in the Pyrenees, about 25 miles (40 kilometers) from Carcassonne in the south of France in the Languedoc-Roussillon region, sits a tiny town with a church and grounds called Rennes-le-Chateau that may hold the secret of the Cathars, and more. The church, which is dedicated to Mary Magdalene and bears the dedication above the front doors *"This is a place of awe, this is God's House, the gate of heaven, and it shall be called the royal court of God,"* was restored from an almost ruined state starting in 1887 at the hands of a mysterious priest, Berenger Sauniere, who, according to legend, found some shocking and enigmatic parchments containing a genealogy that could shake the foundation of human history. He found them after moving a heavy altar stone inside a hollow pillar. One of the messages allegedly translated by Sauniere was "A Dagobert II Roi et a Sion est ce tresor et il la mort," which translates to "To King Dagobert II and to Sion belongs this treasure, and he is dead there." Later, Sauniere was in Paris, where he purchased a reproduction of an intriguing painting called *The Shepards of Arcadia* originally painted by Nicholas Poussin in 1640. The painting depicts three shepherds standing near a sarcophagus upon which is the inscription "Et in Arcadia, Ego," which means "And in Arcadia, I."

Figure 6-1: The Shepars of Arcadia by Nicholas Poussin is said to contain secret symbols and signs as to where the tomb of Christ is located.

This sarcophagus was said to be buried somewhere near Rennes-le-Chateau because of similarities in the featured terrain and may have been the burial place of Jesus. And the genealogy Sauniere found at the church ruins site may have been Christ's lineage, the "royal bloodline," the "san graal" or Holy Grail itself, showing the line of holy offspring up to the Merovingian dynasty of the Franks.

One of the groups responsible for keeping these secrets—well, secret—was another "secret society" called the Priory of Sion, referring to the "Sion" mentioned in the enigmatic writings Sauniere found in the hollowed out pillar, and written about in modern pop culture books like *The Da Vinci Code* by Dan Brown and the non-fiction *Holy Blood, Holy Grail* by Henry Lincoln, Richard Leigh, and Michael Baigent, among many others that have cropped up since.

The Priory was an alleged sect that may have been behind the creation of the Templars, and was said to exist to guard the secret of all secrets, this royal bloodline and all involved. Initiates of the Priory who achieved Grand Master status may have included the likes of Da Vinci himself, Sir Isaac Newton, Victor Hugo, and other such luminaries who devoted their lives to protecting the descendants of Christ and the Magdalene. However, the entire Priory may have been nothing more than the wild creation of one Pierre Plantard in 1956, an anti-Semite and member of a minor occult group himself, who forged the fake order in a series of letters found dating from the 1960s to try to set himself up as the next Grand Master of the Order. Whether or not Plantard was fictionalizing fact, or making the whole thing up from scratch, people continue to believe the legend of the Priory and their connection to the secret treasure.

But let's get back to that painting. The fact that Jesus might be buried near the church site at Rennes-le-Chateau, and the potential existence of treasure deep below the bowels of the church floors, again made even more popular by Dan Brown's novels and other books making similar claims, has led to a constant influx of researchers, tourists, and treasure seekers. As of yet, no treasure has been discovered, and no sarcophagus matching that of Poussin's painting—and yet, the Church holds many symbolic secrets that may one day give up the location of what so many seem to be seeking the truth.

Henry Lincoln, a researcher and author who has devoted a great deal of time to the history and mystery at this site, believes that sacred geometry played a distinct role in the building and design of the church site, including hexagons, pentagons, and triangles that can be drawn around the landscape. He cites that this can be done anywhere, of course, but that here at Rennes-le-Chateau, the precision of measurement is so specific it could not be random, as he documented the locations of specific churches related to the legend. He also found that the nearby mountain peaks of Blanchefort, La Soulane, Bezu, Serre de Lauzet, and Rennes-le-Chateau created a perfect pentagon, with La Pique at the dead center point. He associated it with the planet Venus, itself associated with the Magdalene, as being a heavenly symbol of the geometric shape below, marking it as a holy place and possibly the location of the tomb of Christ.

Some claim that the sepulcher of Christ painted by Poussin didn't exist until 1933, and that no tomb existed on that spot prior to that, but we must point out that assumes these researchers actually *found* the right spot. To this day, there is still incredible controversy over whether any of the legends of this locale are true or fabricated, yet one has to wonder why a tiny, sleepy place would want all the attention from noisy, nosy tourists—and we all know now that even myth and legend have, at their core, a nugget of truth.

Still, regardless of whether Sauniere found any treasure, or whether he created the whole story to make himself richer and bring money to his little part of the world, or whether Jesus and Mary Magdelene ever were married and their lineage documented on parchment and guarded by secret knights of God, the main church, and the Tour Magdala, which was built on the edge of the village and used by Sauniere as a library, continue to suggest that Mary was far more than just some harlot Jesus tolerated on his preaching route. It suggested that, to some, she was a woman of incredible importance, to be revered and worshipped of her own right, for reasons that still elude us but are found in clues in the Nag Hammadi, Rennes-le-Chateau, and in the history of the Cathars, Templars, and the alleged Sion. Though no excavations in the area have turned up anything like a treasure, and the bloodline documents are nowhere to be found, the legend persists. In fact, because of pop culture it has grown. But again, we have to ask: Is there a grain of truth here, hidden deep within the fictional elements, yet there nonetheless? Why was a whore so important as to become the central figure of such legends? Things that make you go "hmm...."

Templar Connection

Another secret society linked with the Cathar treasure and pos-sibly the bloodline of Christ is the Knights Templar, also known as the Order of the Temple, the Poor Fellow Soldiers of Christ and of the Temple of Solomon, and sometimes just plain old Templars. This medieval order was a powerful group of dedicated Christians who took on a military role and even fought in the Crusades, their flags embla-zoned with the now-famous red cross on a white background. They had their own infrastructure and secret initiations, and ruled supreme, with the Church's blessing, for two centuries, but they also had alleged asso-ciations with the protection of the bloodline of Christ and the Cathar secrets, which would have made them double agents.

Yet the Templars are often portrayed as monks who became mil-itarized to protect Christian pilgrims that were traveling from Jaffa, a port city in Israel, to Jerusalem, and were said to have discovered the legendary treasure buried at King Solomon's Temple, which they then took under their protection. They got very rich, very quick, and that got the current king, Phillip IV of France, very suspicious and angry because he was said to be indebted to the Templars himself. So with papal blessings from Pope Clement, he ordered their arrests as a way to take possession of their riches. The Templars were rounded up on Friday the 13th of October in 1307 (which later became associated with the superstitions surrounding "Friday the 13th"), tried, and tortured into confessing to all sorts of charges, including homosexuality, and many were burned at the stake, including two of the leaders of the Order. Their assets were seized, and those who survived were sent packing to other regions or were absorbed into an existing military order called Order of Hospitallers. Portuguese Templars were smart; they escaped and simply changed their order's name to "Knights of Christ" to avoid further papal scrutiny.

Legend has it that one Templar leader, Jacques de Molay, who was burned at the stake, cursed both Pope Clement, who ordered the arrests, and King Phillip. One month later, Pope Clement passed on, and King Phillip IV died shortly after of a hunting accident.

Later Templar groups were closely linked with Masonic teachings and were not directly connected to the Middle Ages version, even though they continued to pattern their rites and order degrees after the original Templars of old. They are now considered a philanthropic, chivalric order, and members share no specific religious affiliation, just a belief in a supreme being. Modern Templars are associated with other groups like the Knights of Malta, Knights of Saint Paul, and the York Rite of the Knights of the Red Cross.

Today, we know of many secret societies of the past and the present that appear enigmatic and mysterious, suggesting they hold knowledge passed down from the ancients that we, the general riff raff, are not privy to. Some of these societies take on a religious or spiritual bent, but others seem more political and power-oriented.

Mannerbund

Though many people suggest these groups are nothing more than a chance for a bunch of men to get together, dress up, perform silly rites, and pretend to be important, the rumors persist of real power, importance, and even the transmission of secrets down family lines. Possibly as a tribute to the original concept of "Mannerbund," or pre-modern warrior societies what were men only, to qualify as a secret society, all you really must do is operate in secret, keep out women (usually, but not always), and have some cool initiation rites and order rules. You might throw in some costumes like robes and strange hats. Some societies actually are in existence to teach knowledge, especially esoteric knowledge, and they do so with very structured lessons and initiation levels a member must go through to learn great truths. Why these great truths are available only to the select few may seem arrogant, but originally could have been to keep the teachings pure and avoid public adulteration of ideas and concepts, which could be kept under control by vetting initiates and novices to make sure they were of the right motive and intent.

One of the oldest student groups is the infamous Skull and Bones, of which past U.S. Bush presidents both belonged to. This is a group, founded in 1832, of elite Yale University students who join and partake of rites and rituals that are inspired by Masonry. They meet twice a week in a building called The Tomb (they were originally known as the Brotherhood of Death) and no doubt plan world domination while their fellow students are out rowing and wooing co-eds. Some conspiracy theorists suggest the CIA is behind the creation of this society, from which they can pick upcoming leaders, or maybe keep an eye on them! A number of colleges and universities sport secret societies, and this also leans toward the fraternities and sororities, and their selective memberships and bizarre initiations.

Other elite secret societies include the OTO, or Order of the Temples of the East, or Order Templi Orientis, a fraternal and religious order founded in the early 20th century, which has some roots in Masonic rites, but the religious beliefs of Thelema, courtesy of occultist and general spokesman Aleister Crowley. The founding principle of Thelema was "Do what thou wilt shall be the whole of the law, love is the law, love under will," but the Gnostic masses created by Crowley were all over the map, often featuring naked priestesses, and invoking Egyptian Gods and even the Devil.

The Hermetic Order of the Golden Dawn, created by three men who were Freemasons, was a magical order based in England during the 19th and early 20th centuries. The founders, William Robert Woodman, William Wynn Westcott, and Samuel Liddell MacGregor Mathers, based their rituals and teachings on Christian mysticism, Kabbalah, the Tarot, alchemy, theosophy, and even ancient Hermeticism, based upon the Cipher Documents that were attributed to Johannas Trithemius. The documents were said to be magic rituals that had a touch of Rosicrucian influence. There were three Orders initiates had to master, each based upon a different level of esoteric or magical philosophy and practice. The Golden Dawn is often considered to have had great influence on later occult groups such as the Ordo Templi Orientis and even Wiccan teachings.

Other more modern societies include the Illuminati and Opus Dei, which are often portrayed in pop culture as evil power-mongers who are out to overtake the world, although for different motivations. They may not have any secrets to pass on except how to control populaces, banks, monetary systems, and real estate, and create a legendary New World Order. Interestingly, the Illuminati originated after the Enlightenment, sometime in 1776, as a group of Bavarian thinkers, intellectuals, and progressives, who did not require any particular religious belief, despite having many Masonic members. Most were humanists, and this may have led to today's conspiracy-oriented portrayal of a modern, powermad Illuminati intent on destroying all religion. The original group probably petered out in the late 1700s when the government attempted to outlaw such groups, but some conspiracy theorists suggest they are still around and more sinister than ever, overseeing every action of every politician, religious leader, and corporate entity on the planet.

Opus Dei got some bad press in Dan Brown's blockbuster novel *The Da Vinci Code,* and is not really out to destroy the Priory of Sion and forever hide from public view the bloodline of Christ. At least that's what they tell us. The Catholic Church formed the organization in Spain in 1928 with Pope Pius XII's approval as an order for those who wanted to embrace celibacy, and a strict and devoted path to sanctity. Whether or not they have higher ambitions, only the order knows for sure.

Our main interest, though, lies in two secret societies that are most alleged to have been engaged in the ritualistic transmission of information, especially spiritual knowledge and truth, over centuries, and continue to do so in the present day.

Rosicrucians

The practice of alchemy, or the transmutation of base metals into gold, may have been at the heart of the origins of Rosicrucianism. Said to have originated in the 1600s, after a series of three published documents influenced a group of German Protestants, the Rosicrucian order is one of the biggest and most influential secret societies in history. The term comes from the name Christian Rosenkreuz, a legendary alchemist who traveled all over the world gathering secret truths and knowledge. The three documents this order was based upon are the *Fama Fraternitatis Rosae Crucis (The Fame of the Brotherhood of RC),* the *Confessio Fraternitatis (The Confession of the Brotherhood of*

RC), and *The Chymical Wedding of Christian Rosenkreutz anno 1459.* The first refers to the story of Rosenkreuz (Rose Cross) as a traveling doctor and alchemist, the second to a secret alchemist brotherhood that sought to change European politics and philosophy, and the third to a chemical wedding of a king and queen at a Castle of Miracles. This chemical wedding was most likely a reference to the strong influence of alchemy in Rosicrucian teachings, but not the alchemy of metals and gold. Rather, this was about the spiritual transmutation of the human into an enlightened soul, which followed a similar process.

Figure 6-2: The Temple of the Rosy Cross is a powerful symbol of Rosicrucianism. This image dates from 1618, by Teophilus Schweighardt Constantiens.

Though original members opposed Roman Catholicism, they were open to both Protestant and Lutheran teachings, and their symbol was the "Rosy Cross" that spoke of Christian mystical influences, as well as Hermetica, the ancient Egyptian-Greek wisdom texts of the second and third centuries AD of the teacher and sage Hermes Trismegistus, which may have been responsible for the high interest in alchemy. The Rosicrucian Enlightenment, as the period between 1614 and 1620 AD was called, saw the publication of hundreds of books and documents heavily influenced by, or critical of, Rosicrucianism. Though many members claim their order is older than Freemasonry, and point to the 18th degree of Scottish Rite Masonry called the Knight of the Rose Croix as proof, that is still up for debate, but the two groups do share some commonalities, including degrees of initiation or membership.

The oldest known Order in the United States is the Fraternitas Rosae Crucis (Fraternity of the Rosy Cross, or FRC), founded by Paschal Beverly Randolph in 1858, which claims roots to the original Fraternity instituted in Germany in 1614. Today's Rosicrucian land-scape is filled with groups that may or may not be directly related to the original, but continue to uphold its main teachings and structure. Though not quite as secret today—there is a Website and anyone can sign up for teachings and trainings, including women—the actual mystery tradition remains a part of our history that turned the tide of thought, art, culture, politics, and religion into a more spiritual, and inner-directed one, for those who chose to follow it.

One of the key teachings of Rosicrucian enlightenment and truth focuses on alchemy, including the pursuit of the formula for the legendary Philosopher's Stone and Elixir of Life, which were the Holy Grail to Western alchemists. The Philosopher's Stone was thought to be a very common substance, perhaps a tincture or powder, as it is referred to in alchemical writings, which could transmute base metals into gold, silver, and other precious metals. This base substance could also be at the root of the Elixir of Life that would render perfect a human soul, cure disease, and bring about spiritual enlightenment. The quest for this stone occupied alchemists throughout Europe during the Middle Ages and into the 17th century; they experimented for days on end in laboratories seeking the elusive substance. Their experimentations served to add to our body of knowledge of chemistry, metallurgy, and even pharmacology, even though none are thought to ever have stumbled upon the Elixir or the Stone.

Alchemical Pursuits

In the Hermetic and later Rosicrucian wisdom teachings, this same process was to be pursued in a spiritual sense and, with the right lessons and training and rites and initiations, one could move up levels of transformation and reach that pinnacle of enlightenment, that inner Philosopher's Stone, and find a powerful Elixir of Life that could do all the same things the physical elixir was alleged to do: give back our youth, make us live far longer, and have far more vigor and verve.

Alchemy is both an art and a science, maybe also a philosophy, then, with roots in all three and is now recognized as a "proto-science" to today's modern chemistry and medicine, albeit one that included an awful lot of mythology, magic, and religion. Unlike today's stringent adherence to the scientific method, alchemy allowed for the inclusion of the hidden and invisible powers and forces at work that could bring about inner perfection even as the outer perfection of the base metals was the visible goal. During the darker parts of the Middle Ages, the practice of alchemy in a laboratory setting gave the sense of a real scientific pursuit, and may have been a perfect deflector away from the mystical aspects under the watchful eyes of authority figures who probably didn't want men learning how to become divine. The devotion to pursuing this alchemical transformation was an obsession to many, but to the church and political power figures at the time it was a dangerous attempt to usurp their own control and make obsolete the religious institutions that insisted one could not know the divine, or be the divine, or achieve truth without the aid of priests and popes and other middlemen.

When it came to the use of alchemy in Rosicrucian teachings, one man was thought to best represent the cause of the spiritual approach to this mysterious science. Thomas Vaughn, a Magus of the Rosicrucian Order, was a 17th-century Welsh adept who wrote many alchemical treatises under the pseudonym Eireneus Philalethes, including the noted *Lumin de Lumine,* which documented how alchemy was a part of physical, mental, and spiritual reality. He wrote of the Quintessence of the Divine Life, an invisible spiritual substance that permeated all of life (think chi or the Force) and all form, and that the Philosopher's Stone was also a "touchstone" that had the power to bring about spiritual transmutation and purify the adept's body and spirit. This substance, which he called "The Medicine," could cure disease and even bring the sick back from the brink of death, and was manifested in every plane of consciousness. To Vaughn, this was the Great Secret, the gold that came from the basest of metals. He wrote in *Lumin de Lumine*, "I have made the Stone, but do not possess it by theft, but by the gift of God. I have made it and daily have it in my power, having formed it with my own hands. I write the things that I know."

His works included other notable alchemical texts, including *An Open Entrance to the Shut Palace of the King,* filled with alchemical symbolism, truth, and scientific discovery, referring in the text again to a "Medicine Universal, both for prolonging life and curing all diseases."

Freemasons

In his book *General History of Freemasonry,* Robert Macoy, a 33rd degree Mason, wrote about the importance of the ancient secret societies and schools as being powerful influences on contemporary intellect and posterity: "It appears that all the perfection of civilization, and all the advancement made in philosophy, science and art among the ancients are due to those institutions which, under the veil of mystery, sought to illustrate the sublime truths of religion, morality, and virtue, and impress them on the hearts of their disciples."

The ancient mystery schools passed down, via their adepts and initiates, the knowledge and truths and keys to wisdom that could help a man find union with the one God, and find beauty and dignity of the soul, as well as the promise of eternal life. Only later in history, when greed and power entered many of these very traditions, infiltrating them, and disrupting and perverting their original true aims and goals, did these secret societies take on a more sinister tone.

Freemasonry has been accused of both.

What was once a loose fraternal organization of stonemasons back in the Middle Ages who were said to meet after working hours to eat and talk in a lodge set up near a particular building site, Freemasonry has gone from small lodges and labor groups to the huge and more philosophical, even esoteric, sprawling entity it is today, retaining its mystery along the way. Though some claims suggest the Grand Masonic Lodge of Freemasonry was created around 1717, others cite Masonic origins as far older, even deep into the Middle Ages when various lodges came together into Grand Lodges in England, Scotland, Ireland, and the United States much later, around 1730, when the first American lodges sprung up in Pennsylvania, spreading beyond the state after the end of the American Revolution.

Figure 6-3: The Square and the Compass is the most well-known symbol of Freemasonry. The G is said to symbolize God, or Gnosis. Image courtesy of MesserWoland.

Masonic rites and traditions may vary a little according to the country of origin, but in general, to be a real, bona fide Mason, you had to be recommended by another Mason and rise through three main degrees: Entered Apprentice—basic membership; Fellow Craft—intermediate degree of knowledge; and Master Mason—necessary for taking part in Masonic activities. Scottish Rite Masonry has 33 degrees. Note the importance of the number three, which was considered a powerful and sacred number in Masonic thought. Masons have their own special signs, symbols, handshakes, and even clothing worn by members, although again these can differ a bit from region to region, and in the original Anglo-American form, exempt women from joining, ban all political discussions and commentary, and demand a belief in a Supreme Being or Great Architect of the Universe. The more liberal Continental Freemasonry does allow women, does allow political discourse, and promotes separation of church and state and religious freedom, even non-belief.

Most Masonic rituals, principles, and activities are the same, though, focusing on the powerful symbolism of stonemason tools as part of the rituals and rites, and the teaching of morals, brotherly love (not sisterly, unless you are in the liberal branch!), virtue, and truth. As a member progresses through the degrees, he learns to be a more moral human being, understands himself and others better, and in general improves his relationship with God, the Supreme Being.

That is the generic description of Freemasonry, but many conspiracies exist that paint a darker picture of the secret society as a powerful entity involved in modern religion, politics, and the future of humanity, and not always for the benefit of the populace. This paints a far different picture of the "operative masonry" of the real stonemasons of the Middle Ages who were artisans and craftsmen.

Ancient Artisans

In *The Secret History of Freemasonry,* author and Freemason Paul Naudon writes of the less-known connections between Masons and Templars, and how both may have originated from the "collegia," or college of artisans, of ancient Rome. The goal of these organizations was the transmission of knowledge and information about a sacred tradition that originated before Christianity, to modern times. This transmission occurred in the rituals, rites, and symbolism of the traditions.

Naudon also cites the ecclesiastical association of builders that were formed by Benedictine bishops in the early Middle Ages, along with the Cistercians and the Templars, as well as trade-based freemasonry as origin sources from which the tradition emerged.

Naudon points out the differences between operative Freemasonry, which was the older and more labor-oriented, and speculative Freemasonry of later times, which adopted more religious and philosophical elements. Rituals and teachings were not written down, and were orally transmitted, making it difficult to pinpoint what was done and what it meant. But many rituals used symbolism said to be associated with sacred geometry, most notably of that of the Temple of Solomon and of Rosslyn Chapel in Scotland, which is steeped in Masonic symbols. The Temple of Solomon, which was begun by David and then completed by Solomon as a worship place of the Eternal One and the house of the Ark of the Covenant and the Tablets of the Law, was thought in medieval times, Naudon writes, as a symbol of God's true temple on both the Universal/Divine plane, and that of Man, who was "the reduced form of the Universe to which Christ's incarnation had conferred a level of grandeur or some value sequel to it. The temple was the symbol of both the universal macrocosm and the human microcosm."

As above, so below—again the Hermetic belief that found its way into many secret mystery schools.

Solomon's Temple

The symbolism of the legend of the Temple of Solomon is key to Masonic teachings and thought. When King Solomon, son of David, set out to build the Temple in the year in Jerusalem in 950 BC, an event described in the biblical Book of Kings, he hired to work with him one Hiram Abiff, who said he knew the secret of the temple. When Abiff was kidnapped and threatened with death if he did not cough up the secret, he refused and was murdered. King Solomon got word of his murder and ordered a group of Masons to search for Abiff's body and the alleged secret of the temple. Legend has it that the Masons he sent were not successful, so King Solomon established a new Masonic secret, believed to be the word *Mahabone,* meaning "the Grand Lodge door opened," a password now used to enter the third degree of Masonry.

"AND he reared up the pillars before the temple, one on the right hand, and the other on the left; and called the name of that on the right hand Jachin, and the name of that on the left Boaz." (II Chron. 17.)

The Temple porch contained two great copper or bronze pillars called "Boaz and Jachin," which were said to have guarded the temple and were adorned with important symbols. Boaz is said to mean "strength," and Jachin, "to establish," and many scholars wonder if these pillars refer to the two kings responsible for the Temple, David and Solomon. These pillars are now often found in reproductions in most Masonic lodges, having taken on a legendary status even separate from the Temple itself.

Rosslyn Chapel

Another rather legendary site to Masons, and to Templars as well, is Rosslyn Chapel in Scotland. Although again steeped in legend, the Chapel was built around 1440 AD by William Sinclair, the 1st Earl of Caithness, a man sometimes said to be of direct lineage to Christ in conspiracy circles, as one of three places of worship in the Roslin, Midlothian region of Scotland. Many architectural features allege a Masonic or Templar influence or symbolism, including the "Master Pillar" and "Apprentice Pillar" at the east end of the chapel, named from a legend of an 18th-century master mason and his young apprentice. The master mason lacked faith that his apprentice could handle the task of carving the column without aid of an original design, but when the apprentice did indeed carve the original design sight unseen, the master got angry and killed the apprentice. As punishment, the master mason's face was carved across the apprentice pillar so the master would spend eternity gazing upon it.

Other symbols such as the hand placements of various figures
depicted suggest Masonic symbolism, as might a carving that shows a
blindfolded man led forward by a noose held by another figure wearing a mantle like those of the Templars, similar to how an initiate is
inducted into Freemasonry. Because the chapel was built in the 15th
century, and earliest records of Masonic lodges date back to the 16th
and 17th centuries, some suggest the Masonic imagery was added later
when known freemasons may have been among the workers hired to
restore the church. Adding to the mystery is another William Sinclair,
who later became the first Grand Master of the Lodge of Scotland and
the first in a long line of Sinclair Masons, but who wasn't the same Sinclair that built the chapel in the first place.

Of course, all of these connections have been questioned and many
even debunked, but the legendary connections continue, thanks in part
to Rosslyn's prevalence in Dan Brown's *The Da Vinci Code* and subsequent suggestions that the Templar treasure was buried under Rosslyn,
along with the head of Christ, the Holy Grail, and other such items that
may have included a piece of the actual crucifixion cross itself. None of
these items have been found.

There does remain, however, an incredible mystery encoded within
the Chapel in the form of 213 protruding stone cubes that are carved
into the pillars and arches with various patterns on them. At the end
of each arch is an angel playing some type of musical instrument. No
one knew the meaning of these cubes, or the patterns they made, but a
father and son team may have discovered their purpose.

The cubes, they say, are a musical score encoded in the 600-year-
old chapel. Tommy J. Mitchell and his son, Stuart, studied the cubes
for 27 years before they found that there were actual tonalities and
pitches that matched the symbols on each cube, creating what they call
a harmonic and melodic progression. The symbols first had to be deciphered and were found by the researchers to be part of the cymatics

music system known as "Chladni patterns," a study of wave phenomena associated with physical patterns produced through interaction of sound waves in a medium.

The "song" the cubes played out sounded to the Mitchells like a melodious nursery rhyme and they named it "The Rosslyn Motet." Though there were no accompanying lyrics to be found that might explain the song, we might recall the common belief of many secret societies and wisdom schools: as above, so below.

Any Great Architect would tell you that the language of the universe is mathematics, which are the force behind harmonics and music.

Masonic History:
Were Our Founding Fathers Masons?

Many of America's most revered "founding fathers" were Freemasons. Benjamin Franklin was a Grand Master in 1734, and edited and published the first Masonic book in America that same year. Thomas Paine, also a Mason, wrote *An Essay on the Origin of Free-Masonry* in the early 19th century. Important historical figures who may have been Masons include Samuel Adams, Patrick Henry, Francis Scott Key, John Hancock, Paul Revere, Elbridge Gerry, Josiah Bartlett, and George Clinton. Even George Washington. In fact, he has a memorial called the George Washington Masonic National Memorial in Alexandria, Virginia, to show for it.

This may explain the ongoing allegations that everything from the shape of the Pentagon to the symbolism of the Liberty Bell to the Statue of Liberty and the American Eagle and the eye and pyramid on the dollar bill all have esoteric, if not downright occult or Masonic, meaning behind them.

But a vast majority of the signers of the Declaration of Independence and the U.S. Constitution were not Freemasons, and had no association with any Masonic lodges. This means that the

Masons were not behind all of the alleged conspiracies they've been accused of, including being the Illuminati engineering the New World Order from dark and smoky backrooms, Reptilians ready to take over the world and install alien rule, and the key power players behind every aspect of governance of these United States.

In fact, much of the architecture and symbolism we see in our great land has other origins, possibly from ancient Greek, Roman, and Egyptian deities and beliefs, or no doubt Christian foundations—heck, even the pagans get represented in the form of the lovely lady who welcomes all into the New World, the Statue of Liberty, which was a gift to us from France and clearly a representation of a pagan goddess with her seven rays beaming out from her crown.

The pyramid on our dollar looks an awful lot like those at Cheops. Not everything is, was, or will forever be a big Masonic conspiracy!

When our ancestors thought about passing on important knowledge, especially that of the esoteric kind, they didn't always have to turn to big secret societies, or large chapels and cathedrals. In fact, sometimes they used very small items that may have seemed insignificant on the surface, or embedded that knowledge in pre-existing knowledge like a palimpsest they hoped no one would notice.

Hidden Images and Codes

The actual art/science of writing hidden messages that only the sender and recipient can see is called steganography, and though this focuses mainly on concealed writing or coded writing, rather than the visible encrypted messages of modern technology, it can also include messages that are in a sense "hiding in plain sight." One of the oldest uses of this art form dates back to 440 BC in the form of a coded warning about an oncoming attack that was written on the wooden backing of a wax tablet before applying its beeswax surface.

Through history, we've learned imaginative ways to hide messages and codes, with secret inks, different typefaces to create a patterned message, tiny codes under postage stamps on envelopes, and even the blinking eyes in Morse Code of American POW Jeremiah Denton, who was able to spell out "torture" during a 1966 press conference and confirm that our soldiers were being tortured in North Vietnam.

One of the most talked about and controversial hidden message systems is said to exist right in the Bible itself.

The Bible Code

Thirteenth-century Rabbi Bachya ben Asher might have been the first to suggest that a type of code called ELS was present in the Torah, an idea later confirmed by other rabbis and then written about in a modern pop culture phenomenon called *The Bible Code* by American journalist Michael Drosnin in 1997. ELS stands for "Equidistant Letter Sequence" and was first publicly presented in 1994 by Doron Witztum, Eliyahu Rips, and Yoav Rosbenberg, who had studied the presence of ELS in the Book of Genesis.

What we now call Bible codes are patterns of letters that are at exact and equal distances apart that create specific words, or phrases, often apocalyptic and prophetic. Found in both the Old Testament and New Testament, these alleged codes could also be displayed simultaneously as an "ELS letter array" by writing out text in a grid with the same number of letters in each line, then cutting it out in rectangle form. You would have to choose a specific starting point and pick a skip number, then select all letters in the text at equal spacing as given by the skip number. So, you could start at the beginning word, and then choose every fifth letter to create your coded message.

Sometimes, ELS can draw out entire sentences with prophetic meaning, which means that the pattern outcome would less likely be a result of sheer chance. The longer the ELS are extended, the more likely you have a real pattern or coded system at work.

Though Drosnin popularized the Bible code with his mass market book and a second one, *Bible Code II: The Countdown* (released in 2002), a number of critical studies and objection experiments showed that ELS could be applied to any book, including *Moby Dick* and *War and Peace,* and eventually a pattern would emerge, thus rendering the Bible messages as nothing more than sheer chance, and not the divine code of the holy book's authors who painstakingly set down the letters in their proper orders thousands of years ago. Drosnin was accused of leaving out of his examples intersecting passages and phrase extensions that would render the ELS code null and void. A group of mathematicians and statisticians even went on record signing a statement saying they did not believe there to be anything valid to the Bible code phenomenon, all of them having examined the evidence at hand and finding it unconvincing.

Regardless, there are still those who believe that the codes in the Bible warned us of assassinations, terrorism, comets and meteors, and even the end times—or it was just another example of people seeing what they wanted to see where they wanted to see it.

Tarot Cards

Tarot cards are another means by which some occultists allege hidden knowledge has been passed on under the radar of religious authorities. The original tarot decks were playing cards from the mid-15th century used to play "tarocchini" in Italy and "tarau" in France. Only after the late 18th century were these cards used as a form of divination, with symbols embedded in the imagery that conveyed a deeper spiritual knowledge to those who knew how to "read" them.

The original decks had 78 cards of four suits with pip cards from ace to 10, and four face cards per suit. In addition, there was a 21-card "trump suit" and a single Fool card, much like our modern "Joker" card. Occultists now call the trump cards the "major arcana" and the suit cards the "minor arcana." Though there is no valid proof of any use of these cards as anything but game decks before the 18th century, some tarot readers will still insist they are much older and filled with ancient knowledge.

The oldest picture card decks date back to around 1420 AD and were first mentioned as a 16-picture card deck with Greek gods, and suits depicting birds, not the usual images we know of today. Motifs and imagery usually involved astronomical objects, animals, poetry, deities, and heroes, with the hand-painted cards of the upper classes often done to portray and celebrate family members. The more occult symbolism began in the mid-1500s when the cards became a form of divination, maybe in part due to the book *The Oracles of Francesco Marcolino da Forli,* which depicted cards used in a simple, oracle-style reading.

A Swiss clergyman named Antoine Court de Gebelin, who portrayed the decks of the Tarot of Marseille specifically as ripe with symbolism of the Isis/Thoth mysteries, didn't apply great magical meaning until around 1781 when the tarot became more associated with mysticism, in part due to the publication of *Le Monde Primitif.* From that point on, future decks were designed with specific themes in mind, such as the highly popular "Rider-Waite" deck, drawn to specific instructions by occultist Arthur Edward Waite in 1901. This deck more than any other is filled with esoterica and occult symbolism, but newer editions have been unfortunately altered and modified, and no longer reflect Waite's true intent.

Even the older Marseilles deck contains imagery that could be used for divining purposes, but the problem is, as with any kind of images and symbols, a matter of personal interpretation. Cards like the Fool or Death are often thought to be negative when in fact they may signify anything but a negative situation. Death cards are said to be about change and transformation, and the Fool, about choices and decisions. One deck focuses on Hermetic philosophies and teachings, called obviously the "Hermetic Tarot," and uses symbolism important to the rituals and teachings of the Hermetic Order of the Golden Dawn as well as Jungian symbolism of archetypes and the realm of the psyche.

The problem is always in the person who looks at these cards and attempts to make an interpretation based upon images and symbols that may or may not have much meat behind them at all. Most likely, these game cards were just that: game cards—and later allowed for a bit of personal expression of ideas that might not have been completely accepted in a public forum. But the tarot remains less a form of transmission of information and more a system of fun, and even divination, that might actually be based upon nothing more than the intuitive interaction of the reader and the one being read for.

Knowledge Gone Forever?

Not to end on a tragic note, but when it comes to hidden information, there is so much of it that will never reach our waiting minds and eyes, not because it is encoded in some form we cannot understand, but because it is gone—simply gone, never to be recovered.

When we try to imagine what knowledge might have been forever destroyed in ancient times, when parts of the Royal Library of Alexandria burned, it boggles the mind and breaks the heart. There are four possible end dates for this vast repository of the world's largest library, dating from fire during the Alexandrian War in 48 BC to the Muslim conquest in 642 AD. Even after the main part of the library was destroyed, along with so much of our past with it, another smaller library that had been set up by scholars at a temple known as Serapeum was also destroyed by fire in 391 AD.

To this day, we cannot know the extent of the holy texts, the wisdom writings and scrolls, the art and artifacts contained in this massive complex that was dedicated to the collection of the world's knowledge. And to think that the library was only a part of the bigger complex, which included a Museum and research center for the study of astronomy, anatomy, biology, and zoology, as well as experiments in physics, mathematics, medicine, and geography boggles the mind with just how vast a body of knowledge we have lost. Though there is much of the museum that has survived, the Roman philosopher Seneca referred to more than 40,000 stored books that burned with the library, and there is incredible debate to this day over what the true extent of the damage might have been.

Still, not every sacred text or holy scroll, body of knowledge or wisdom teaching, mystical tradition or esoteric learning system has been lost, and to this day we are still given the task of trying to figure out which of what remains is truly ancient in origin or the result of "add-ons" through time. And then there is the hope, too, that one day, the Vatican in Rome might open up its vast archives of documents, artifacts, texts, and information to the public eye, although that date seems somewhere way off in the future, if ever. And we can only wonder at the secrets held in those basement vaults and secret archives that are said to contain 52 miles of shelving and 35,000-plus volumes in the selective catalog, not to mention the yet-to-be-indexed materials, all of which are forbidden to us (qualified scholars can see some of the content, after going through a vigorous clearance process), yet hinted at in modern novels and movies that speak of world-changing mysteries of the highest order. Game changers. Shift shapers.

As this book is being written, antiquities in Egypt are being destroyed in the violence of political and religious uprising. It's a shame, because the anger of today is literally wiping out the knowledge of yesterday. So we are left to sort through the information that comes to us via the surviving pathways and try to understand what they, our ancestors, wanted us to know.

Chapter 7

Outsourced:
Ancient Aliens, Invisible Fields, and Other Outside Information Sources

Aliens!

—Giorgio Tsoukalos, on the hugely
popular History Channel
show *Ancient Aliens*

According to StatisticsBrain.com, in 2011 more than 2,273,000 American jobs were outsourced to other countries. (No information was available for 2012.) Of the CFOs surveyed, 35 percent said they outsourced jobs, with 24 percent favoring China and 18 percent favoring outsourcing to India.

There is so much talk over jobs, and information, such as banking and medical records, being sent overseas to places where the work needed can be done faster, cheaper, and easier. Most CFOs cited reduced costs as their main goal, but a whopping 38 percent went to outside countries for research and development, and 49 percent did it to gain access to information technology and management ideas and innovations not available "internally."

There are people who believe we may have gotten a little outsourced information of our own a long time ago, a little help with advancing our knowledge, science, and technology from our friends, only not in other countries...but on other planets.

Ancient Astronauts and Aliens

The ancient astronaut/alien theory is a simple one: Through time we have been visited by aliens, who have changed, shifted, altered, and advanced our own limited civilization. Although academically, this theory is not accepted, if even entertained in general, it has become an idea for our time, thanks in part to the very successful History Channel show *Ancient Aliens,* which has exposed these ideas to millions of viewers.

Talk about taking it viral.

Yes, we in the past have had our *In Search Of,* with Leonard Nimoy narrating, but the History Channel scored a viewership coup with the program that features a variety of writers, researchers, and even a few skeptics discussing the possibility that our advancement was outsourced to the stars.

Though we are not writing a book about ancient aliens—that has been done by so many other writers—we do want to look at this particular theory in general as a means of possible transmission of information. Is it valid? Does it make sense? Can we prove it? Yes, maybe, and no.

The theory also proposes that the gods, goddesses, and other deities of old religions might have actually been aliens, but were described as gods because of the limited knowledge of the people at the time (although why believing in an alien is more "advanced" than believing in a deity has never been explained well enough), who did not truly know how big the Universe was and how many possible habitable planets might exist. Of course, this is to deny the power of the imagination, for we have to stop here and ask if our ancient ancestors didn't envision science fiction stories in their heads just as we do today in books, TV, and movies.

But, let's get back to the theory.

Might we even be descendants of alien? Whereas this book desires to focus on the transmission of knowledge and information, the idea that we either have alien DNA or were created by aliens could indeed change the way we think of our own capabilities. Some ancient astronaut/alien believers think that aliens altered the course of evolution, or that they genetically engineered humans and that would account for the gaps in evolutionary theory. But for now, let's go with us being perfectly human. Occam's razor, you know?

Ancient astronaut theorists suggest that the only way big leaps in advancement in our progressive civilization could have possibly occurred was via outside help—the help of advanced civilizations that were not anywhere to be found on earth. Thus, they must be star people who took on the responsibility of coming to earth, helping us out intellectually, and leaving behind objects and things out of place and time such as those we discussed in an earlier chapter, including legends and stories of their visitations, before going back to the stars from whence they came.

Some of the proponents point to biblical stories of giants among men, the Nephilim of the Book of Genesis who were said to be "sons of God" who mated with human women, and mentions of chariots in the sky like those witnessed by Ezekiel in the Old Testament, and objects like the Hindu *vimanas,* or flying cars that sound very much like aliens and their craft. They also point to glyphs and drawings throughout various ancient cultures of helmeted men, winged beings, and bizarre craft-like objects spewing fire behind them.

Is It Proof?

Although all of this could be called evidence of ancient alien visitation, also referred to as "paleocontact," and to those who have made a living out of the study, research, and writing of just such a thing, this is at most circumstantial evidence, not outright proof. The key players in the ancient astronaut/alien theory are not entirely new, possibly having their start, as so many alien concepts do, in the science fiction of the late 19th century on, before becoming a subject for real serious study.

We are not talking UFOs here, or close encounters of the first, second, third, or any other kind. What we want to understand is whether or not there is any real evidence of validity to the idea that humans could not have been responsible for the leaps of transmission of information, not to mention the quality of the information. Dozens of books have been written on the ancient astronaut/alien theory—most pro, a few balanced, not many skeptical. The skeptics have remained somewhat silent, with a couple of serious scientists speaking out at the inconsistencies of the theory's key aspects, and a few Christian-leaning videos, blogs, and articles approaching the theory from their own limited belief system. One of the debunking sites did absolutely nothing to disprove the entire theory, while successfully picking apart specific claims, such as a stone figure wearing a clearly animal-headdress that the show claimed was an alien astronaut "helmet," neither did it offer alternative explanations that might have made more sense about the claim overall.

One bit of debunking "proof" was to suggest the Nazca Lines couldn't have been used as alien runways, as suggested by some ancient alien proponents, because the surface is made up of a shallow trench of sand from which darker colored pebbles have been removed to create the pattern, and by the chaotic display of lines that might have confused even the best pilot. *True.* Any craft "landing" on the trench would no doubt destroy it. But they fail to explain why the objects were etched into the landscape in the first place, which could have been simply, and probably were, to honor or revere sky gods, either bird or otherwise, something we do today when we build churches and holy sites of worship. These lines are not proof of aliens, and they are not proof of "not aliens." They are mysterious lines we will never truly understand because we weren't there to directly question those who put them there. And *that* is the only truth we have to hold onto, no matter what side of the fence we are on.

Some of the debunkers do make great points of poking holes in the interpretations of the proponents of the theory, and succeed in identifying fraudulent and fake statements that come from misinterpretations of holy texts, images, and symbols, and follow up with alternative possible explanations. But many of the debunkers have no background in archeology, anthropology, history, mythology, or comparative religion, and instead either settle for personal attacks on the people involved, bash television shows in general, or make huge assumptions of their own, and ask us to believe them without evidence to back it up—which is exactly what they claim the proponents are doing. Just as we ask our readers to use discernment when reading up on this subject, we ask them to have equal discernment reading the debunkers. Though we agree with the debunkers that not every unknown can be attributed to "aliens," we certainly don't deny that perhaps some can.

Unfortunately, until a cadre of real and credible academics and scientists get together to answer all these questions, the questions remain open for interpretation, no matter how flawed either side may see it.

So, most of the rest of us are stuck with, again, bits and pieces of information, some of it no doubt able to be interpreted one way or another depending on the motives and agendas of the sources.

The television series features a variety of proponents of the theory, including wild-haired producer Giorgio A. Tsoukalos, who has become a meme due to the success of the program and often gives way more airtime to believers than to those who challenge the theory. Still, we must remember it's a television show, and the authors of this book you are reading know full well that you can be interviewed for a show for hours and only have small bits of your discussion used on the program, which rarely tells the entire story, and that anything on television is usually done for entertainment over education. But, as many debunkers would have us believe, does that mean everyone on the show is a fraud? A liar? Nope, not at all. Many of the guests on the show are legitimate scientists, authors, and researchers with a vast body of work behind them in archeology, archeo-astronomy, geology, anthropology, history, and other fields that have a vested interest in identifying how information and knowledge progressed along the historic time line. We authors have heard some of these guests speak at conferences, away from TV cameras, where they have shown amazing evidence for their claims, and also openly stated they did *not* have all the answers.

Does this mean we authors believe in the theory ourselves? We do, and we don't. And that is our job—to examine all the various possibilities with as open a mind as we can, while understanding the bigger picture, as earlier chapters of this book point out, of how information reaches us and is often encoded in what we deem "fiction."

Sadly, there is so much negative discourse now; a real honest and straightforward dialogue might be impossible. Like in politics, once people take sides, it's hard to sway them back to center. In fact, we strongly encourage our readers to read up on materials from both sides and make their own decisions. A mind is a terrible thing to waste.

Okay, we shall set off of our proverbial soapboxes now.

Major Theory Players

The theory itself, though, is based on a body of work that includes books by notables such as Erich von Däniken, author of the block-buster 1968 *Chariots of the Gods,* a controversial book that led to many sequels and a ton of controversy when it came out, especially from religious fronts who took offence at the content. Scientists and academia basically poo-poo-ed the book, but von Däniken earned a growing audience as he continued to write and speak about the two main kinds of evidence he and others were looking for: clues found in ancient holy texts and ancient artwork, architectural sites like the pyramids, and mysterious out-of-place objects that suggested we humans once interacted with beings from the sky.

Von Däniken is often called the grandfather of the ancient astronaut/alien theory, but others have contributed to the debate and discussion as well, including Harold T. Wilkins, who wrote books about flying saucers, the mysteries of time and space, and the secret cities and ancient mysteries of South America way back in the 1940s and 1950s; Charles Fort, an American researcher into anomalous phenomena, for whom the term *forteana* was coined, in the late 1870s through the early 1930s, and who wrote a book that he never published about Martians controlling events on earth before writing *The Book of the Damned* in 1919 about "damned data" or paranormal phenomena that science rejected; Robert Temple, who wrote a book in 1976 called *The Sirius Mystery* that set off a firestorm of interest into the West African Dogon tribe and their amazing knowledge of the cosmos, that he claimed were comparable to the beliefs of both ancient Egyptians and Sumerians; and Zecharia Sitchin, an Azerbaijani-born American author who claims to be one of few scholars permitted to read and interpret ancient Sumerian and Akkadian clay tablets, as his Website states, and who focused his books and research on the ancient Sumerian civilization and their links to the Anunnaki, a race that inhabited the planet Nibiru orbiting out beyond Neptune, who came to visit Earth more than 400,000 years ago to look for gold, and, in an attempt to genetically create miners to help them, created the human race instead, including the "Adapa," equated with Adam of the Book of Genesis. Sitchin's work includes a series called *The Earth Chronicles,* starting with the "12th Planet," which told the story of Nibiru, and ending in 2007 with "The End of Days: Armageddon and Prophecies of the Return." He wrote numerous other books as well, including his last book before his death in 2010, *There Were Giants Upon the Earth: Gods, Demigods, and Human Ancestry: The Evidence of Alien DNA.* However, his publisher, Bear & Company, will release a novel Sitchin was said to have been writing in secret before his death titled *The King Who Refused to Die: The Anunnaki and the Search for Immortality,* said to be an allegorical story based on his actual research.

Newer books include one we believe to be very objective and worth reading, among all the others we suggest here and the Bibliography: author and researcher Philip Coppens's *The Ancient Alien Question: A New Inquiry Into the Existence, Evidence, and Influence of Ancient Visitors.* Coppens sadly passed away recently, but the body of work he left behind is instrumental to a solid understanding of lost civilizations and ancient knowledge. A very new book, *Aliens in Ancient Egypt: The Brotherhood of the Serpent and the Secrets of the Nile Civilization* by Xaviant Haze introduces some new and cutting-edge information about the alien question. We strongly suggest reading the older books, the newer books, and everything in between, including a collection of essays and articles about lost civilizations by New Page Books called *Lost Civilizations and Secrets of the Past,* which features a variety of contributors and insights, because this is a huge puzzle with many pieces spread out over a variety of arenas of academia, science, and religion.

There are many others writing and speaking about the ancient astronaut/alien theory, and we don't wish to slight them, but we don't want to focus either on the theory itself; it's been dissected enough. Most approach the subject from the study of ancient Egypt, because of its tremendous advancement, which seems to have happened almost overnight, in science and physics, medicine and astronomy, and art, almost as if someone came along and tutored them. There seems to be a rift between orthodox Egyptologists and those of a more ancient alien bent, over everything from who built what, how they built it, and why.

Many of these proponents point to the pyramids at Giza, Easter Island's Moai statues, Stonehenge, and Avebury, and other massive monuments and edifices, and incredibly old and sophisticated sites like Puma Panku near Tiwanaku, Bolivia, or Gobekli Tepe in Turkey, or the Star Child skull and its alleged non-human DNA, and the Abydos helicopter (all subjects we strongly suggest you look into, pro and con) as proof of alien intervention; we say hello baby, call me maybe. All of these monuments and sites defy rational explanation and even challenge our assumptions about how old human civilization really is—but are they proof of alien architectural consultation or assistance? Not necessarily. Many people suggest we couldn't have possibly raised the megaton blocks that build the pyramids, or moved the giant stones that created the henge monuments, or cut to the finest paper-thin perfection the slabs that served as the foundations for temples and sanctuaries unearthed and revealed. Yet, why couldn't we?

Other Ideas

New theories involving sonic levitation, made even more credible with scientific research and experimentation involving the use of sound waves to lift small objects, as well as existing theories involving lifts and pulleys and pure mass labor, appear to hold just as much weight (pun intended), yet we are so drawn to the easy way out, which would be aliens dropping from the sky with the technology that allows us to whip up a pyramid. Yet we cannot seem to find evidence of that technology. Did it die with our ancestors, or is it encoded in their stories and myths and religious texts? Where are the blueprints to the machines—the long manuals with instructions on how to cut a chunk of stone to a precise measurement?

Biblical scholars might point to the details of the building of the Temple of Solomon included in the Old Testament text, and archeologists point to tiny passages and tunnels deep inside the pyramid that only a small alien could wiggle through (why not a dwarf or a child?) and we hear bits of clues about messengers from above giving instructions to mortal men to build a ship, a craft, a temple, a monument; all are valuable clues to try to piece together our past, if we interpret them correctly.

Even then, there would still be so many questions, because some codes are impossible to break without the actual key.

Again, we turn to the question of whether or not alien intervention, despite the many people citing circumstantial evidence of it, would even be needed to help humans along the evolutionary road to higher knowledge, consciousness, and innovation. One of the ways we might get a better perspective on this is to step out of the past and think about the present.

One of the disadvantages our ancient ancestors had was the lack of computers, cell phones, and ways to not only write down mass amounts of information, but pay it forward as well. Our future descendants will no doubt appreciate the sheer volume of facts and events we've recorded for them to one day decipher and learn from—and yet, what if they advance so much that even with all the paperwork and proof we leave behind, they still don't understand it? Isn't it possible that this simple explanation could account for why today we have such a hard time truly deciphering the symbols, art, glyphs and images, stories, songs, and myths of old?

Some say that it had to be aliens, or something that helped us make leaps in advancement we didn't appear ready to make. But again we point to the state of technology today, and the amazing progresses we have seen just in the last 100 years, when we "leaped" forward from books by firelight to toting our Kindles on our flight. We had no television 100 years ago. No spaceflight. No computers. No cell phones. Yet here we are in a blink of the eye with all that and more on deck, including holograms of rock stars, curing diseases with sound waves, quantum computing, and possible 7-11s on Mars.

It took great innovative and imaginative minds to make those leaps throughout time. Henry Ford, Steve Jobs, Bill Gates, Nikola Tesla, Ben Franklin, Alexander Graham Bell, Marie Curie, Thomas Edison, and Steve Wozniak, and whoever the person was that invented Pop Tarts— these were people who had the foresight and ability to think outside of the box and because of it, we leaped.

Unless, of course, you believe they were all aliens!

Overnight Success

It is highly possible that those very same leaps took place thousands of years ago, over short bursts of time, but to us today seem to have happened overnight. We think here of "overnight success" stories of celebrities, athletes, writers, and so forth. To the public, the success of someone like J.K. Rowling, the author of the Harry Potter empire, might seem to have happened in a flash. Yet Rowling knows of the years leading up to the big break, and the hard work that we did not see because they were not being lived under the microscope of public view. Our ancestors could indeed have made huge leaps that appear to us, now, as overnight successes, yet took decades—maybe even centuries—to build up to. When tipping points come, they come fast, but the progress toward the tip could take much longer. Even if it is only a year, think about how your own life can change drastically in just 365 days when you make one change, or one choice, or one discovery that alters every aspect of the way you live.

The bottom line is this: Whether we believe in alien intervention, access to a field of all information, completely natural human innovation, sheer imagination, or some troll named Joe who showed up one day thousands of years ago with a blueprint of the future, no one will ever truly know how things went down for one reason, and one reason only: We weren't there. And as of yet, no one has discovered an operator old enough to call and ask for "information, please?"

We hate to say only time will tell, but perhaps it's only a matter of time before a site is excavated or a text is discovered that provides enough detail and maybe even a few more that can corroborate it, that tells us how we got from there to here.

Is it possible that ancient people had other means by which they could access information and ideas that did not exist at the time? Or at least didn't exist within their own culture?

Collective Data Bank

Swiss psychologist Carl Jung wrote extensively about the collective unconscious, the part of the human mind that is common to humanity as a whole and is distinct from our personal consciousness. This collective mind, if you will, contained memories and archetypes, which were universal images, symbols, dreams, and ideas understood by all cultures that represent the basic human experience. The collective unconscious, which Jung actually based on experiences he had observing and working with schizophrenics, has also been called a "universal dumping ground" or "data bank" for all information, past, present, and future. The information in the collective unconscious is given to us at birth. We don't have to "learn" it; it comes with the territory, and is inherent to the brain.

Jung himself said in *The Structure of the Psyche:*

The collective unconscious—so far as we can say anything about it at all—appears to consist of mythological motifs or primordial images, for which reason the myths of all nations are its real exponents. In fact, the whole of mythology could be taken as a sort of projection of the collective unconscious.... We can therefore study the collective unconscious in two ways, either in mythology or in the analysis of the individual.

Yet this collective data bank—this field of information from which our personal psyche and consciousness tapped into for that information we did not ourselves have direct experience with—might be the storehouse of ideas that our ancient ancestors tapped into as well.

Archetypes, as we wrote about earlier, manifest in the stories and images of not just mythology, but religious writings as well, and they also play a huge role in our own personalities and behaviors. Jung believed that the collective and its archetypal images served as a king of transcendental wisdom that all of humanity had access to that went above and beyond that of everyday conscious experience. He also suggested that the causes of synchronicities were embedded in the collective unconscious, with the effects visible in the conscious realm.

Perhaps some of the visions and encounters written about in the Bible and other texts, believed to be aliens offering wisdom and knowledge and information, may instead have been angels, entities, and other beings speaking to people via the collective unconscious, archetypal beings appearing in dreams bearing the gifts of wisdom and ideas. The gods and deities and winged creatures may have indeed been Jung's concept of symbolic beings designed to appeal to us on a much deeper level than the conscious mind could understand. The blueprints for pyramids, henges, and monuments could have been transmitted via the collective mind, from the great data bank and universal information field to individual minds eager and ready to receive such information.

Maybe that's how ideas and stories and innovations work today, as many writers have attested to the sense of being channels for the work, and not the actual originators. Even today, we all know of certain ideas, especially in the entertainment industry, that suddenly seemed to be everywhere at the same time, as if suddenly 20 different people got the urge to write about a cannibal named Louie who lived on a small island off the coast of Greenland. We chalk it up as coincidence or just copycat lack of originality, but if all the information that ever existed was contained in this field—this data bank—would it not be possible for two different civilizations to suddenly get the same light bulb idea at the same time, even though they were thousands of miles away?

❦

Laird Scranton is the author of *The Science of the Dogon: Decoding The African Mystery Tradition,* and is one of the leading authorities on the West African Dogon and their cosmology, which is filled with stunning symbols and concepts similar to the most cutting-edge science. We talked with him about where this native tribe may have gotten their advanced knowledge.

In your research into the Dogon, you have found amazing commonalities between their worldview and cosmology and the most cutting-edge science of today. How do you believe they "got" the knowledge that they did?

LS: The belief of the Dogon priests is that their system of knowledge was imparted to them in ancient times as a kind of civilizing plan by knowledgeable teachers. The Dogon cosmological tradition is a close match for the cosmology associated with a Buddhist *stupa,* and the Buddhists overtly credit the most "sacred" aspects of their knowledge to a "non-human source." (See Adrian Snodgrass, *The Symbolism of the Stupa,* p. 3.)

We see often such similarities in symbols, imagery, art, architecture, myths, and origin stories among ancient cultures that could not have possibly been in communication with each other the way we are today, with computers and the Internet and social networking. How do you think knowledge, wisdom, and information "went viral," and was transmitted in ancient times?

LS: If we go back far enough, this same belief in knowledgeable teachers seems to lie at the heart of many different ancient cultures. Based on that fact, it looks to me as if the knowledge was deliberately imparted in widespread regions, in an effort comparable to what the modern-day Peace Corps does in underdeveloped countries.

Evidence suggests that cosmology typically preceded written language in ancient cultures, and was transmitted from generation to generation by way of a system of mnemonic symbols, themes, and ritual practices—essentially Jung's *archetypes.* My research suggests that many of these symbols and their associated concepts were later adopted as the drawn symbols of the earliest written languages. For example, the base plan of the aligned *stupa* shrine, which derives from a stick with a circle drawn around it, defines the shape of a sundial—the same shape that came to represent the sun in the hieroglyphs of Egypt, Tibet, and China.

In support of these viewpoints, I see widespread commonality of important cosmological symbols and terms from culture to culture about 3000 BC, and in how those symbols and concepts carry forward into written language. Cosmological shapes were often employed in very similar ways in the earliest written languages of these cultures. For example, a 10-day week was observed, both in ancient Egypt and in ancient China. In both cultures, the word for *week* was written with symbols that convey the meaning of "ten days."

Week   ⊙ ∩   A day [⊙] ten times [∩], or "ten days" (The ancient Egyptians observed a 10-day week) *(See the word met. Budge p. 331a)*

In retrospect—and contrary to expectation—the earlier system of mnemonic symbols might be seen to have been a more effective mode of transmission of information than the later written word—comparison of similar cosmological traditions suggests that the cultures that did the best job of preserving their tradition were those such as the Dogon, who never actually implemented a system of writing.

Laird Scranton, a software designer from Albany, New York, is the author of two books on African and Egyptian cosmology and language. His focus is on the study of comparative cosmology, which is the study of the classic myths, symbols, deities, cosmological concepts, rituals, and words of various ancient and modern cultures. His emphasis has been on defining fundamental similarities between the cosmologies of the modern-day Dogon tribe of Mali, ancient Egypt, and Buddhism. His recent studies have extended to the cosmologies and hieroglyphic languages of Tibet and China, with focus on the creation tradition of the priestly Na-Khi tribe. His current project is writing a book on ancient Chinese cosmology and language.

Fields and Grids

Science points to the Zero Point Field, a quantum sea of potentiality and infinite information from which all form and matter and energy come from and return to, which we've written about extensively in our earlier books and which may be equated with the religious kingdom of heaven—which is described as continuing everything within, yet invisible and all around and through us. Other similar terms come to mind: the Akashic Field, the Book of Life, the Sea of Quintessence, Morphic Fields, and, as we authors call it, the Grid. All of these are theories that involve a "grand, ground source," as physicist Hal Puthoff once put it, which is the foundation of everything, according to *The Field:*

The Quest for the Secret Force of the Universe by Lynne McTaggart. This source, which later George Lucas equated with his Force in the *Star Wars* movies, is a sea of quantum superposition, where everything is waiting to be given form and structure, but exists until then as nothing but potential, or probability. We prefer to envision it as a Grid, because of the multi-dimensionality of our Universe, which theoretical and quantum physicists talk of when they discuss "the multiverse," "parallel universes," "M-branes," "alternate dimensions," and "bubble universes."

Theoretically, we exist in many of these other worlds, experiencing different time lines.

In our many books, we've discussed our visual idea and ongoing theory of the potential infrastructure of reality, which might look like a three-dimensional Grid and contain within it all there was, is, and ever will be, including different levels of reality we might actually be experiencing when we have a mystical, religious, or paranormal encounter. The Grid, like the Zero Point Field, the Akasha, and the Kingdom of Heaven, is invisible, but, as with gravity, which is also invisible, we see the effects and influences of its presence all around us. We just cannot see the cause, at least not in our conscious reality. The collective unconscious operates the information in the Grid, which we access when we have an intuition, inspiration, hunch, or creative idea, or even when we find the solution to a problem we've been struggling with. We have this infinite field of timeless wisdom and information to tap into, this quantum sea of potentiality and possibility in which all choices—even the ones not taken—exist.

Again, the Grid cannot be seen, but its influences and effects can be seen and experienced all around us, as our personal reality, and as the collective reality, and all other realities above and below and beside. We jump from level to level when we dream, get inspired, intuit something, create, and a host of other ways that perhaps our ancestors did as well to access wisdom and knowledge.

So this Grid, filled with every idea and bit of information possible, every it and bit necessary to become a tree or a cat, build a car or a pyramid, photosynthesize, or engage in single cell division—because, again, it is that eternal data bank of wisdom as Jung suggested—could be the inspiration behind one man's idea to build a huge monument to honor a God or Goddess, or a living human like a pharaoh. And, just as all of the innovators and creators and inventors of today, they did what no one else thought possible at the time. They, he, or she built the damn thing.

Maybe the ideas came from the imaginations of men and women, and that is as simple an explanation as we can offer. Ideas spread via word of mouth by travelers, or throughout region after region until an entire continent catches on. They spread in writing and song and symbol. We dream ideas and often access information in dreams that is understood on a subconscious level. Sometimes we dream something into being or dream a solution or an invention or a story plot.

We think that ancient cultures were sophisticated because they had advanced knowledge of this science or that field of medicine, yet we forget that many of these cultures were still, at the very same time, sacrificing humans and children to Gods and Goddesses, and anthro-pomorphizing everything in sight, not to mention engaging in strange and primitive rituals and rites that give away their lack of all-around knowledge and understanding. You can be brilliant and stupid at the same time! Today, we see amazing and brilliant minds coming up with ways to travel to Mars and rove about the landscape, create computers that are smaller than our fingertips and almost as fast as the speed of light, build skyscrapers that touch the heavens and bullet trains that link cities, and all sorts of mind-blowing innovations—and yet we are still going to war; killing each other; engaging in intolerant, racist, sexist, homophobic behavior; abusing animals and children and the environment; looting and pillaging and raping. As advanced as we like to think we are, perhaps our future offspring will look back at those behaviors and label us primitive.

So it is possible to make huge leaps in science and architecture, medicine and art, and every other good thing while still being a very backward culture as a whole. Understanding that, here again we ask: Are aliens necessary for great leaps in growth and knowledge? Could we have done it on our own simply by being receptive to the potential ideas that were out there to anyone daring enough to think outside the box? And all those stories and images of what sound and appear to be aliens wearing helmets and strange craft zipping about the sky—could our ancestors have actually seen just that, or were they seeing something they couldn't understand and trying their best to describe it, and the onus of responsibility for interpreting it right or wrong is off them and on us?

Or were they dreaming and envisioning archetypes that existed deep within their psyches, then sharing them with anyone who would listen?

There is a ton of evidence to support the ancient astronaut/alien theory, and evidence to debunk it. There is a ton of evidence to support the Field/Grid theory, and evidence against it. There is a ton of evidence to support good old human ingenuity, drive, and ambition, and evidence counter to it.

If you ask us, the only way to know for sure is to invent a time machine, go back thousands of years, and look with our own eyes. When that becomes possible, we'll write a book on it. (Wait a second— we already did!)

Aliens or ??? Look at the following three artifacts. Evidence of ancient aliens, or something else? Turn to page 242 to see what these are!

Figure 7-1: Image courtesy of WikiCommons.

Figure 7-2: Image courtesy of Richard Croft.

Figure 7-3: Image courtesy of DedaloNur.

Chapter 8

The Stories of Our Lives:
How Today's Ideas Will Become
Tomorrow's Viral Mythology

You ask me if I keep a notebook to record my great ideas. I've only ever had one.

—Albert Einstein

It is not once nor twice but times without number that the same ideas make their appearance in the world.

—Aristotle

Citizens of the nation: I shall not try to conceal the gravity of the situation that confronts the country, nor the concern of your government in protecting the lives and property of its people...we must continue the performance of our duties each and every one of us, so that we may confront this destructive adversary with a nation united, courageous, and consecrated to the preservation of human supremacy on this earth....

—From Mercury Theatre on Air,
War of the Worlds, 1938

On Sunday, October 30, at 8 p.m., something happened that would send people all over the country into a panic. The year was 1938, and a radio broadcast came over the airwaves that would shock its listeners into running for the hills—well, those who weren't able to tune in from the start and hear Orson Welles say that he, on behalf of the Mercury Theatre on the Air, was about to present *War of the Worlds* by H.G. Wells, for their listening pleasure. The broadcast was done in a serious tone, with intense music and official sounding news bulletins. But many listeners tuned in a bit later, when Welles was past the introduction and deep into Wells's story of a Martian invasion on U.S. shores—and took it seriously.

Nuttiness ensued.

Thousands of people called into their local radio stations, police stations, and newspaper offices. Many people in the New England area actually loaded up their cars with kids and a few goods they could grab, and fled the region. People flocked into local churches to pray and await imminent death. There were alleged reports of people having heart attacks, miscarriages, and early births. The panic was widespread as more and more people became hysterical, thinking the Martian invasion was real.

Once word got out that it wasn't real, and was just a pre-Halloween radio show meant to entertain, people became outraged and threatened to sue the program, and many people expressed their anger at Orson Welles for causing the panic.

But what had really happened was something that happens all the time: People got a piece of information, made an assumption before getting all the information, and reacted accordingly.

Mob rule. Hysteria. Riots in the streets. Contagious panic. Collective fear.

As popular singer Adele might have sang during the chaos, "Rumor Has It...."

Cut to 2013 and all over the Internet, across social networking sites like Facebook and Twitter, the story is spreading like wildfire of an actual angel dressed in priestly clothing that turned up out of thin air at a terrible auto accident, and blessed the victims before helping rescue workers. Then he vanished into thin air, just the way he arrived. Everyone was flummoxed. Who was this mystery priest—this unidentified angel? The word *angel,* in fact, was everywhere, even before people took a breath long enough to wait for the real story to emerge.

There really *was* a real priest there at the scene. He just didn't want a lot of fuss made over his actions. His name was Reverend Patrick Dowling, from the Diocese of Jefferson County, Missouri, and he just did what God would have expected of him: He absolved and anointed the victim, 19-year-old Katie Lentz, and then got out of the way to let rescuers do their job. Simple.

Just a few months before that, it seemed the entire nation was waiting breathlessly, anxiety mounting, collectively frenzied as social network sites BLEW UP with news of its coming—waiting and waiting, posting and waiting—until finally the moment came, when the SyFy Channel aired the premiere of *Sharknado,* starring Tara Reid and Ian Ziering, and a host of other less-than-B-list stars. The 90-minute movie was awful, to say the least, but it didn't matter, because so many people tuned in that a sequel was ordered immediately. (In the original, the sharknado destroys L.A. The sequel moves to New York. Watch out Chicago—you're next.)

But it wasn't the movie that is important here. It did, indeed, suck so badly, it would have scored a negative 10 on the list of the 10 worst films ever made. What was so utterly stunning to watch was the absolutely insane hype that spread like wildfire over Twitter and Facebook—any marketing firm's dream—causing record-breaking numbers of posts that some say should have been reserved for major world events, like assassinations of presidents and terrorist attacks. Though it is highly doubtful that the next *Sharknado* will have that same effect, now that the novelty has worn off. But why?

Why did so many people buy into the viral spread of this ridiculous campy motion picture?

Going Viral

In the case of viral ideas, there may indeed be reasons why certain ones thrive, while others can barely survive.

When Malcolm Gladwell's highly influential *The Tipping Point* (see Chapter 1) set the marketing world on fire, talking of the importance of "influencers" as the responsible parties for the contagious spread of ideas and innovations, he may have left a big chunk out of the viral equation. A newer book, published in 2012, called *Everything Is Obvious: How Common Sense Fails Us* by Duncan J. Watts, a professor of sociology at Columbia University, posits that influencers are not anywhere near as important as the receivers, the audience, and for an idea to go viral, that audience, especially when it comes to social networking, has to be enthusiastic or approving of the idea presented. And, he argues, rarely does common sense enter the picture.

Watts found that although influencers are one end of the yardstick—and are indeed responsible for igniting the match that sets an idea viral and makes it contagious—what allows it to spread like wildfire is the receptivity of the people who then post, tag, spread, share, and endorse. If they collectively do not respond, the idea could hit a wall. So whereas Watts, in his research, does admit that highly influential people are more likely to trigger a social epidemic, it's the receptors that make or break it, and the more easily influenced those receptors are, the wider the idea spreads. Often, subject matter, timing, and the topic of the idea or innovation counts as much, too, as an idea may go viral, but again may hit a wall at some point if the subject isn't one that has widespread appeal and the ability to evoke collective enthusiasm (or repulsion, as what goes viral isn't always positive; just see the spider bite posts on Facebook to know what we mean!).

So, why do some ideas take on a viral quality and others fall by the wayside?

It may be all in the presentation, and the power of persuasion. Say you are a vacuum cleaner salesman. You go door to door, trying to sell your product by telling people all its good qualities and how this hose is better than the old hose, and the floor settings contain two new ones over last year's model, and look—it comes in green, too. You sell one or two if you're lucky. Your colleague goes door to door and instead asks if their cat has ever emptied its food bowl onto the carpeting, or if the lady of the house has ever dropped coffee grounds on the floor, and then sets out to "solve a problem" by telling all the reasons why the vacuum can make the customer's life so much better. He or she sells 10 in one day.

One tries to sell on common sense, the other on emotional and personal impact.

Getting Contagious

According to Jonah Berger, assistant professor of marketing at Wharton School of Business, there are specific ways to make an idea or any kind of content or information viral, and the secret is in getting contagious. In a research paper he wrote with Katy Milkman called "What Makes Online Content Go Viral?" Berger came up with the following:

1. Positive content is more viral than negative content. Yes, even in today's environment of "if it bleeds, it leads," we tend to spread further those things that make us feel better.

2. Content that evokes *any* high arousal emotion is more viral than content without emotion. If it makes you feel something, whether fear, anger, or joy, and feel it strongly, you are more likely to respond, repost, re-tweet, and repeat.

3. Practical and useful content gets shared. If it is something that someone needs to do something better, easier, cheaper, more fun, or more efficiently, it goes viral more often.

Content, therefore, is not always "king" unless it meets the parameters by which it can be shared with larger groups of people, over wider networks. Certainly, our ancient ancestors shared with each other, and through time, with us, *what was important to them,* whether because they found it useful, it evoked emotion, or made them feel better. Or, they passed down what they were persuaded to by someone who could talk up a good storm full of passion and emotion and reasons why they had the information that counted.

We pass on certain pieces of information, and ignore others we deem not important or fit to spread around. We might even do this because of our brains.

A recent neuroscience study set out to prove why some ideas go viral and others fall by the wayside. What is it, the researchers asked, that makes an idea—which is, remember, information—buzz worthy? In the study, as documented in a *Forbes* article titled "Your Brain on Buzz: Why Some Ideas Go Viral and Others Go Nowhere" (July 6, 2013), a group of UCLA students were presented with 20 or so ideas for a potential television show while hooked up to an fMRI brain imaging machine. They were asked to pretend they were interns and evaluate the ideas to pitch to TV producers. Another larger group of students were told that they were the TV producers and watched the same videos of potential show ideas as the first group, then make their evaluations of which ideas were best.

The idea was to see any differences in the brains of those "interns" who most effectively pitched the ideas and those who were not as successful in getting the "producers" to buy the ideas. The scans of the brains showed indeed that the interns who enthusiastically pitched and were the most persuasive had significantly more activity in the temporoparietal junction when they chose their favorite ideas than those who were not successful and enthusiastic about their ideas. This difference in activity was labeled the "salesperson effect" and showed that once a "buzz-worthy" idea hits the brain, a sort of "buzz alarm" goes off and tells the person that this particular idea or piece of information is one worth spreading to others.

"Once that happens," reporter David DiSalvo writes, "the recipient of the idea becomes a better evangelist for its replication, thus increasing the likelihood that the idea will become 'contagious' for the next set of brains." Maybe this is how information not only goes viral, but stands the test of time throughout the course of history, dictating which ideas are passed down to future generations and which ideas are discarded and rejected. If our ancestors had a brain buzz over a certain image, idea, innovation, or invention, it got top priority in their various modes of expression, and managed to survive the passage of time as it was transmitted down the ancestral totem pole to those of us today who are now excavating the information in story, song, art, symbol, and structure.

The only thing that has changed through time is the amount of opportunities we have to go viral, with today's technology, via texting, e-mailing, social networking, radio shows, television, motion pictures, books, magazines, and so forth. But the reasons some ideas survive may always be a part of human nature that doesn't change over time. Get them in the gut.

Other elements have been identified that pinpoint why certain videos go viral over such sites as Facebook and YouTube. Surprise is a big one. If you can surprise people with images or content, they tend to remember it longer and desire to tell someone else about it, in hopes of getting that same surprise response. Even the intensity of the message counts, because we all respond more to people who are telling us something with passion behind it. Relevance and importance always count, as everyone wants to be the purveyor of news, bad or good. Notice how fast news headlines spread over social networking?

Today, everyone watches video clips, and many people even live by them, learning new skills, laughing over funny scenes, and getting personal insight into other people's lives. Unfortunately, too many people look to YouTube videos as their news sources or for "truth," only to be met by just as much, if not more, shaky and un-sourced information as that our mass media presents.

Bad Information

Misinformation, which is just false information that gets spread by accident or lack of oversight, is everywhere. People take something that has not been sourced or proven true, and they spread it, and nobody along the way takes the time to check into the validity, until someone does finally question the viral wave and stop it in its tracks by looking for the real story. At the same time, we are being exposed to everything from disinformation, which is the purposeful spread of false information often by authority figures, to propaganda from our government, the media, and corporations that want us to think and believe one thing over another for their own motives and agendas. Though talk of conspiracies always leads to many a rolled eye, the thing is, we are not being given all the information all of the time, and we end up passing down to future generations only what we have been told.

But is it true?

"Propaganda is neutrally defined as a systematic form of purposeful persuasion that attempts to influence the emotions, attitudes, opinions, and actions of specified target audiences for ideological, political or commercial purposes through the controlled transmission of one-sided messages (which may or may not be factual) via mass and direct media channels. A propaganda organization employs propagandists who engage in propagandism—the applied creation and distribution of such forms of persuasion."

—Richard Alan Nelson, *A Chronology and Glossary of Propaganda in the United States,* 1996

We authors talked with Ron Patton, publisher of *Paranoia Magazine* and producer of the ParanoiaCon Conference about how what we hear isn't always the truth—or close.

How is disinformation used today to influence what information goes viral?

RP: Disinformation, which is the intentional method of disseminating false or inaccurate information, is used primarily via the Internet and media. Since the populace is so enraptured with social networking, it's becomes a viable outlet for spinning such propaganda. The objective is to create spurious theories that appear cogent and believable, but are in fact, unverifiable. Congruently, misinformation is a derivative of disinformation, whereby the tainted data is unintentionally spread by unwitting secondary parties.

During the great world wars, propaganda played a huge role in swaying the populace against the enemy. What role is propaganda playing today in our lives? Who is perpetuating it?

RP: Propaganda is used exponentially, congruent to such technologies as television, computers, cell phones, etc. There's a greater capacity to manipulate the minds of the masses with "information overload." Too much information may cause confusion or desensitization. Again, the mainstream media are the major culprits employing such methodologies. This began systematically, with Operation Mockingbird. This was the CIA campaign beginning in the 1950s, to influence the media by strategically placing agents within the major news networks. The major objectives are: 1) to create fear and induce panic, thereby immobilizing a susceptible public; 2) utilize ad hominem attacks, by unjustly challenging the credibility of a person, organization or movement; and 3) altering historical facts by slightly altering or fabricating factual historical information. "Containment" is also used by intentionally withholding important facts with regard to a particular issue.

What is twilight language and how does it influence ideas and information presented to the public? An example of a recent event utilizing this?

RP: The Twilight Language is derived from Tantric origins; meaning, "secret language." It was regarded as an esoteric tradition of initiation. Conspiracy researcher and author James Shelby Downard expanded the concept in a contemporary perspective, by examining hidden meanings and synchromystic connections via onomatology (study of names), toponymy (study of places) and numerology (study of numbers). Downard regarded it as, "the science of symbolism." Loren Coleman, author of the book *The Copycat Effect*, has meticulously analyzed the recent traumatic events, such as the Aurora and Sandy Hook mass shootings. He also made some startling connections regarding the Boston Marathon bombing. The most glaring was the date—April 19. He states: "This is a time of high violence dates of April 19 (Waco and Oklahoma City bombing anniversaries) and April 20 (Hitler's birthday and Columbine). April 19th is the anniversary of the deaths occurring at the end of the Waco events and the Oklahoma City bombing. It is an older anniversary of the Revolutionary War, of militia deaths, and past school violence incidents."

When it comes to viral information today, how do cognitive dissonance and Hegelian dialectics fit into shaping public perception?

RP: Hegelian dialectics is comprised of a three-stage development: a thesis, giving rise to its reaction, an antithesis, which contradicts or negates the thesis, and the tension between the two being resolved by means of a synthesis. Modern day conspiracy theorists David Icke and Alex Jones have simplified the model by referring to it as "Problem- Reaction-Solution." Cognitive dissonance is a denial mechanism when an idea or belief conflicts with our paradigm or worldview. This is readily evidenced within our two party political system—Republicans and Democrats. Although they contrast, ideologically, the outcome regarding critical policies are essentially the same, with the minor exceptions. Since most people think in a linear fashion, this "smoke-and-mirrors" methodology is ideal from keeping those peripherally impaired from thinking "outside the box."

Conspiracies are often based upon truth, just as smoke often means a fire is present. How do we learn to find the truth in the conspiracy theory?

RP: First of all, most people need to understand the meaning of conspiracy, which is basically a secret plan by a group to do something unlawful or harmful. This has occurred incessantly from the beginning of human existence, and, within all parts of society: religion, politics, business, and families. Once we become more adept in looking at the "big picture" while incorporating deductive and inductive reasoning, we overcome incredulity and semantics, thus, make better sense of the complexities inherent within the array of conspiracies.

Rumor Has It...

So, could the ancients have been victims of the same? Could they have passed on to us their own misinformation, disinformation and propaganda, which we now take as truth and as valid parts of our historical past? The truth is, selective information will always be a challenge for those who wish to understand the past, just as one day people will wonder what our lives were life and what was important to us based upon the information they have available. We all know the power of rumor and gossip. In *A Psychology of Rumor,* written in 1944, author Robert Knapp analyzed more than one thousand rumors spread during World War II that were originally printed in the *Boston Herald*'s "Rumor Clinic" column. Knapp defines rumor as:

> A proposition for belief of topical reference disseminated without official verification.... So formidably defined, rumor is but a special case of informal social communications, including myth, legend, and current humor. From myth and legend it is distinguished by its emphasis on the topical. Where humor is designed to provoke laughter, rumor begs for belief.

His analysis suggested three categories of rumors (along with our own version of what that might look like today):

1. Pipe dream rumors reflect public desires and wished-for outcomes (e.g., Japan's oil reserves were low and thus World War II would soon end). Today's version would be rumors of terrorism finally being over because all members of Al-Qaeda had been killed.

2. Bogie or fear rumors reflect feared outcomes (e.g., an enemy surprise attack is imminent). Today's version would be the media stating that gas station lines were imminent because of a fire at a refinery.

3. Wedge-driving rumors intend to undermine group loyalty or interpersonal relations (e.g., American Catholics were seeking to avoid the draft). Today's version would be the media suggesting people stay out of cities for fear of race riots after a racially charged court case verdict is read.

Knapp discovered that negative rumors were more likely to go viral than positive rumors—which, remember, is the opposite of viral contagion of ideas, which are usually more prone to go viral if they are positive. However, keep in mind that if negative rumors incite fear, they will pack far more emotional punch. Today's rumor mill often involves celebrities, athletes, and politicians and their wrongdoings, which the public seems to salivate over, as well as racially and ethnically charged news items that might incite violence or angry reactions. During a presidential or congressional election, rumors fly on all sides, leaving the confused public picking out what they think is right and true from a sea of misinformation, disinformation, and propaganda to boot.

Remember memes from Chapter 1? Richard Brodie said in *Virus of the Mind* that "When you sell people a bunch of memes, it can program them to spend the rest of their lives behaving the way you want them to." Recall the old saying, that there are *three* sides to every story: yours, theirs, and the truth.

Back in 1938, with only radio as a means of transmission, a story mistaken for fact—a rumor, if you will—caused widespread chaos and disorder. Imagine what can happen today with the modes of communication we are privy to. We saw some of that possibility in 2001 after the 9/11 terrorist attacks, but since then, social networking has exploded, and an event of that magnitude today could literally cause a global panic unlike anything we've ever experienced. Again, we got a taste of that in the days before December 21, 2012, the alleged end of the world/Mayan Calendar. Nothing happened—but if it did, we can only guess at how the information going viral would have changed the world, even if most of it was based on nothing more than assumption, rumor, fear, and hysteria.

Maybe another question to ask is: What are we, right now, creating that will one day become the viral mythology of our times?

There are two main categories of information we are creating today that will be passed on to our offspring:

1. Personal. We leave behind our personal lives in the form of letters, sticky notes, e-mails, texts, stories (oral and written), posts, and pictures on our social networking sites, our clothing, books, music, hobbies, the homes we lived in, our furnishings and art, our body art such as piercings and tattoos and makeup, our creative endeavors whether writing or painting or knitting, our genetics via physical and behavioral traits we pass on to our children, our cars and modes of transport, the food and drinks we consumed, the technology we used, and things we purchased for fun or practical use, including books, DVDs, toys, games, home décor, gardening, and pet care—and even the trash we accumulated and left.

2. Collective. We as a people leave news headlines and stories, social networking sites, trends and fads, cartoons and comic books, and television shows, movies, and books we loved and preferred enough to make blockbusters or bestsellers, our neighborhoods, our parks, our beaches and natural settings, our restaurants and libraries and architecture, our music celebrations and festivals, our art shows and museums and playhouses and strip clubs and casinos, our guns and our flags and our peace signs and protest signs, our rock stars and media stars, and the people we worshipped and made celebrities, our churches and mosques and temples and pagan circles, our airports and train stations and subways and space station.

You get the picture. *Everything* we engage in as a society, as human beings, locally or globally, gets embedded and encoded as pieces of our historical puzzle for someone to put together one day. All of it is infor-mation, from whom we elected president to which nations went to war to who hosted our Olympic games, what laundry detergent brand we favored in 2011, and what we chose as our favorite reality show on TV in 2013. It all counts and will one day all be accounted for.

We still don't quite know why the pyramids were built, or by whom, or who killed John F. Kennedy, or whether or not the government knew about UFOs back in 1947 or do now. Some clues will evade us no mat-ter how hard we dig for them, or evade us so long that we die before we get enough information to answer a particular burning question. Not every piece of information survives the trip over time—and of the its and bits that do, it isn't all necessarily going to make sense to a culture that has no real reference points to work with, other than those that come from educated guesses and putting together a partial puzzle with what pieces we do have.

Future Excavations

Say, for example, a thousand years from now, students excavating at a site in what to us was New York City come across five things: a stash of pornographic magazines, a cache of Kit Kat wrappers, a Tool T-shirt, a copy of *The Catcher in the Rye*, and a souvenir eye patch from a pirate ride at a local amusement park. With those items, which by then will be considered artifacts, the students must create a scenario that connects the dots, and offers a bigger and more complete vision of "a guy from New York City in the 21st century." Yet how much infor-mation is missing? If they also dig up his computer or cell phone and can somehow figure out how to retrieve his texts and e-mails, they will get a better and more rounded view of who he was; and if they happen to find remains of his tiny apartment, the one he paid through the nose for to live in the Big Apple, along with some of his clothing and furnish-ings, those students may be able to draw a decent conclusion as to what he was like and the kind of life he led.

But still, so much will be missing.

That's the problem we face when trying to find, and then interpret, the ideas and information of the ancients: So much is still missing. We study and research and make very educated guesses and often we actually nail it pretty close, but still, so much is missing.

With the ease by which we today can communicate over global distances, instantaneously, thanks to cell phone and computer technology, and the ease by which we can expand our little corner of the world all the way to the four corners via social networking sites that let us befriend people we never would have contact with before, there is a growing, and exponentially growing at that, body of information that someone will have to eventually weed through. God bless 'em.

They, the ancient ones, left us marks on a cave wall, and edifices and monuments, and old texts and scrolls, many of which are missing huge segments. They left us songs and art and churches and stories. They gave us what they had and what we got was simply that which survived long enough. And we do the best we can to make sense of it.

Because in the end, information is king, and the more that we have to work with, the more we know.

Conclusion

There's a story behind every find. A human story...
—Doctoral candidate Shlomit Bechar to CNN
after the discovery in August 2013 of an
Egyptian sphinx unearthed in Israel

As cold as it might seem, we really are nothing but bundles of information, interacting with other bundles and creating new information to be conveyed and expressed to those around us, and to future generations. Our entire lives are meant to inform others as to who we are and who we want to become, not just as individuals, but as a collective—as a species.

Perhaps the ancients, from primitive times forward, utilized all of the theories and ideas suggested in this book as a means of spreading their ideas, their beliefs, and the stories of their lives. Perhaps each theory is a piece of the puzzle of who we were and who we have become. Maybe information spread in all these ways, and others we haven't thought of, simply because we don't entirely know the motives and agendas of those who left these clues behind. We can only guess, based upon our own experiences and ideas, what they might have wanted to tell us, and to show us, with their legends and their art and their architecture.

Ironically, we may have come full circle in the way we express information, as pointed out recently on a social networking site by author/researcher Laird Scranton:

> Evidence in many cultures shows that cosmology preceded written language, and the cosmology was cast in mnemonic symbols and symbolic acts, by which concepts came to be associated with images and objects. Later, when written language was implemented, many of these pre-defined shapes and their associated concepts seem to have been adopted wholesale as written glyphs. But, in fact, our own society has come back around to the point where symbols represent word/acronyms such as NBC (National Broadcasting Agency) or CIA (Central Intelligence Agency).

Funny how what goes around comes around.

Information is like a snowball rolling down a hill, picking up more and more snow as it descends, growing bigger and bigger all the time. Information spreads, adapts, adopts, regroups, shifts, changes, morphs, adds, edits, deletes, and even hides itself at times, but it always manages to keep on rolling down that hill, even as we struggle to properly interpret it. Then again, maybe we should be blaming our mothers, and our grandmothers and their grandmothers, for who we are and what we believe. In an article titled "Grandma's Experiences Leave a Mark on Your Genes" (*Discover Magazine,* June 11, 2013), writer Dan Hurley documents the meeting of two young scientists, Moshe Szyf, a molecular biologist and geneticist, and Michael Meany, a neurobiologist, who got into an animated conversation about genetics while in Madrid and ended up 20 years later enmeshed in the study of how our ancestors' experiences could genetically pass on to us, influencing our own behavior and altering the epigenetic expressions of our genes in the brain.

Meaney had looked seriously into how rearing habits of mother rats might cause lifelong changes in their offspring in ways that in laboratory studies could actually be quantified. When he met Szyf, the two of them ended up performing a series of experiments with mother rats that were either attentive or inattentive. When their pups had grown into adult rats, they then examined their hippocampus regions where the stress response is regulated, and found some stunning differences in the genes that regulate sensitivity to stress hormones, which were more methylated in the neglected rats than those who were under the care of attentive moms. The team went on to perform additional experiments to back up their findings, which continued to show that the epigenetic changes that occurred in the rats' brains had a direct link to how they were raised and how their parent rat behaved. Their landmark paper, "Epigenetic Programming by Maternal Behavior" was published in 2004 in the journal *Nature Neuroscience,* and in dozens of papers afterward, proving that baby rats can gain genetic attachments based entirely on their upbringing.

The team went on, in 2008, to publish a paper comparing the brains of people who had committed suicide with those who died suddenly of other causes, finding the same changes in the hippocampus region that they saw with rats raised with neglect or stress, with the excess methylation of genes.

Can we then, because of these stunning studies, say that we should blame all our bad behaviors, habits, and brain patters on our moms, or any of our ancestors? Even studies with orphans showed the same excess methylation, so it can't just be bad-mommy syndrome driving the development of human behavioral evolution. The same team continues to pile up the studies showing similar epigenetic changes, suggesting that there is really something to the idea that epigenetic changes to genes active in specific brain regions are behind our emotional and intellectual capacities.

Still, we are more than our reactions to stress, and more than our built-in behaviors and how we choose to express, learn, and pass on knowledge. We still, despite the behaviors of our ancestors, can change and evolve and get therapy. The transmission of knowledge is not entirely dependent up on how we feel, or behave, under any specific circumstances, and is only one more piece of the puzzle.

No matter how many clues our ancestors have left us, we still cannot find that one precious final puzzle piece that will complete the picture of our past, simply because we weren't there to witness it firsthand. And that is the most frustrating thing—unless we can all go back in time to the birth of an idea, to the birth of knowledge, and literally ask the individuals in question *why* they wrote the myths and told the tales, *why* they built the pyramids and henges and edifices, *why* they etched the glyphs and chose the symbols, *why* they worshipped the deities they chose, *why, why, why* they did any of the things that have come down the historical pike to us today, we will never truly know.

It is up to us to figure out how to interpret that information once it works its way down.

Today we have the potential means to go to Mars and set up a human colony, and yet we still struggle to truly understand what the primitive peoples were trying to tell us with their rock art, their petroglyphs, their symbols, and their structures. We still struggle to identify the one solid answer to the questions of why ancient cultures built their edifices and monuments the way they did, why they told their myths and stories, and what they wanted us, their distant offspring, to know about who they were and what their place was in the cosmic scheme of things.

Long ago, people sat around fires and told stories. Long ago, people used images to try to express complex thoughts they didn't yet have the words to describe. Long ago, people built things to do more than just create shelter and protect themselves from the elements; they built things to honor the skies and the earth and the seas and the Gods and the deities they believed in and revered. Long ago, people looked at nature and, not yet understanding the science behind it, made up amazing and fantastical stories, legends, and lore to describe what they were seeing.

How much different is this than what we do today? Today, we sit around our cell phones and look at silly images. We watch TV huddled together as breaking news stories unfold. We listen to radio and sing songs we all know the words to. We go into a darkened theater and lose ourselves in a movie, or we escape into the world of art in a museum. We continue to use information not only to experience the world as we see it, and to expand upon that experience, but also to add our own chunks of snow to that ever-growing snowball that will one day be our mark upon the historical landscape.

Will we be remembered one day for *Sharknado* at the same time excavations dig up evidence of rioting and looting after a major disaster? Will car bumpers be dug up by the future archeology students, only to reveal that we "Brake for Garage Sales," that "Jesus Is Coming...Look Busy," and that "My Other Car Is A Broom"? Will scholars of tomorrow find ancient Led Zeppelin T-shirts alongside newer Juicy brand yoga pants, Justin Bieber posters and Taylor Swift lunchboxes buried with sports team memorabilia and video game boxes, *Star Wars* Halloween costumes and *Star Trek* toy phasers, Grumpy Cat calendars and *Duck Dynasty* baseball caps, *Playboy* magazines, and Jenga and pet rocks and Barbie dolls and Legos, and wonder if these were critical to our way of life and who we were as a collective?

Novels like *Moby Dick* will sit alongside *50 Shades of Grey* in museums of the future, where Kindles will be on display next to Droids and iPhones as representations of our crude and primitive forms of communication. (One thousand years from now we will no doubt be talking telepathically!) Old broadcasts of *Lost, The Office,* and *American Idol* will be viewed with great scrutiny, along with movies like *Get Shorty,*

Pulp Fiction, Out of Africa, and *Dawn of the Dead.* Our computers and cars and bullet trains and McMansions, our cars and motorcycles and clothing and accessories, our makeup and toiletries and jewelry and tattoos—all will serve to tell someone, someday, about *us,* as representations of who we were as individuals, and as a species.

Just as we look back at the writings, symbols, art, and architecture of yesterday and try to understand where we came from, we leave a constant trail of clues today as to who we are. The Nike logos on our shoes, the McDonald's arches on tons of trash in our landfills, the IBM and Mac and Microsoft marks on our technology—all will be examined under curious eyes one day.

Yet none of those things will tell a complete story of who we were, and most of it will be open to the interpretation, however correct or incorrect, of those future generations who may, by then, be so far advanced that they cannot comprehend how we survived such a crude existence. We don't think much about the trail we leave, because we are too immersed in living our lives. We leave what we leave, which is exactly what our ancestors may have done. With the exception of secret societies and individuals devoted to making sure certain pieces of knowledge and information got passed on to future generations, most people probably didn't give it a second thought.

Maybe we should be a bit more concerned with looking at what we are leaving behind for this point forward, lest we be thought of as the most primitive and uneducated culture of them all. But maybe we should focus instead on making sure our lives are well lived, no matter the trails we leave, or the clues we plant for some future Nancy Drew or Indiana Jones to mull over. Maybe we shouldn't sweat the small stuff.

Our civilization will hopefully be remembered for the bigger things, the greater things we have achieved: space travel, running water, eradication of major diseases, achievements in science, literature, art, medicine, and education, cutting-edge technology, telescopes that see into the cosmos, particle colliders that peer into the hidden quantum world....

Throw in a few hilarious cat videos, and we are one hell of a culture for those who will come after us to try to understand and learn from.

They will sift through the legends and stories and art and symbols and buildings and monuments and all that we have left behind, and look for clues to try to discern the truth of why we did what we did in the way we did it.

And they will wonder.

Answers to the three alien images questions from Chapter 7

Image 7-1	A female figurine from 500 to 800 AD from Teotihuacan, Mexico. Image courtesy of WikiCommons.
Image 7-2	A Medieval foliat head carving of the Green Man set in the west wall of the St. Michael's church. Image courtesy of Richard Croft.
Image 7-3	A giant Bronze Age sculpture called the Giant of Monte Prima in Sinis, Sardinia, Italy. Image courtesy of DedaloNur.

Bibliography

"Ancient Graffiti Sheds Light on Daily Life." *Archeology News Network,* April 19, 2013.

Baer, Drake. "Harvard Professor Finds That Innovative Ideas Spread Like the Flu: Here's How to Catch Them." *Fast Company,* 2013.

Balter, Michael. "Prehistoric Painters Planned Ahead." *Science Now,* October 13, 2011.

Brodie, Richard. *Virus of the Mind: The New Science of the Meme* (Carlsbad, Calif.: Hay House, 1996).

Brunvand, Jan Harold. *The Study of American Folklore: An Introduction* (New York: W.W. Norton and Co., 1998).

———. *The Vanishing Hitchhiker: American Urban Legends and Their Meanings* (New York: W.W. Norton and Co., 2003).

Bullfinch, Thomas. *Bullfinch's Mythology* (New York: HarperCollins, 1991).

Campbell, Joseph. *Myths to Live By* (New York: Bantam Books, 1978).

———. *The Power of Myth* (New York: Doubleday, 1988).

———. *The Way of the Seeded Earth* (New York: Perennial, 1988).

Christy-Vitale, Joseph. *Watermark: The Disaster That Changed the World and Humanity 12,000 Years Ago.* (New York: Paraview Pocket Books, 2004).

Coppens, Philip. *The Ancient Alien Question: A New Inquiry Into the Existence, Evidence and Influence of Ancient Visitors* (Franklin Lakes, N.J.: New Page Books, 2011).

De Santillana, Giorgio, and Hertha von Dechend. *Hamlet's Mill: An Essay Investigating the Origins of Human Knowledge and its Transmission Through Myth* (Boston, Mass.: David R. Godine, 1992).

DiSalvo, David. "Your Brain on Buzz: Why Some Ideas Go Viral and Others Go Nowhere." *Forbes,* July 6, 2013.

Dundes, Alan. *Folklore Matters* (Knoxville, Tenn.: University of Tennessee Press, 1993).

———. *Interpreting Folklore* (Bloomington, Ind.: Indiana University Press, 1980).

Eliade, Mircea. Translated by Philip Mairet. *Images and Symbols* (Princeton, N.J.: Princeton University Press, 1991).

Eliade, Mircea. *Myth and Reality: Religious Traditions of the World* (Long Grove, Ill.: Waveland Press, Inc., 1998).

Elliot, Alexander. *The Universal Myths: Heroes, Gods, Tricksters and Others* (Harrisburg, Va.: Meridian, 1976).

Frazer, Sir James George. *The Golden Bough* (New York: Touchstone, 1922).

The Folk Lore Society. "First Annual Report of the Council," featured in *The Folk Lore Record* 2, No. 1, 1879.

Frazier, Kendrick, Editor. *The Hundredth Monkey and Other Paradigms of the Paranormal* (New York: Prometheus Books, 1991).

Godin, Seth. *Unleashing the Ideavirus* (New York: Hyperion Books, 2001).

Halpern, Derek. "Creating Viral Content? The Secret is Get Contagious." *SocialTriggers.com,* June 2013.

Hamilton, Edith. *Mythology* (Boston, Mass.: Little, Brown and Company, 1942).

Hancock, Graham. *Fingerprints of the Gods: The Evidence of Earth's Lost Civilization* (New York: Three Rivers Press, 1996).

Haze, Xaviant. *Aliens in Ancient Egypt: The Brotherhood of the Serpent and the Secrets of the Nile Civilization* (Rochester, Vt.: Inner Traditions, 2013).

Hieronimus, Robert, and Laura Cortner. *The United Symbolism of America: Deciphering Hidden Meanings in America's Most Familiar Art, Architecture, and Logos* (Franklin Lakes, N.J.: New Page Books, 2008).

Hurley, Dan. "Grandma's Experiences Leave a Mark on Your Genes." *Discover Magazine,* June 11, 2013.

Jacquet, Jennifer. "How Culture Drove Human Evolution: A Conversation With Joseph Henrich." *Edge Magazine,* 2012.

James, E.O. *Creation and Cosmology: A Historical and Comparative Inquiry* (Boston, Mass.: Brill Academic Publishing, 1997).

Jarus, Owen. "Visible Only From Above, Mystifying Nazca Lines Discovered in Mideast." *LiveScience,* September 2011.

Kenyon, J. Douglas, editor. *Forbidden History: Prehistoric Technologies, Extraterrestrial Intervention and the Suppressed Origins of Civilization* (Rochester, Vt.: Bear & Co., 2005).

LaViolette, Paul A. *Genesis of the Cosmos: The Ancient Science of Creation* (Rochester, Vt.: Bear & Co., 2004).

Lockett, Dr. Michael. "The History of Storytelling." From *The Basics of Storytelling, www.mikelockett.com,* 2007.

Lynch, Aaron. *Thought Contagion: How Belief Spreads Through Society* (New York: Basic Books, 1996).

Lynn, Dr. Heather. *Anthrotheology: Searching for God in Man* (Midnight Crescent Publishing, 2013).

Naudon, Paul. *The Secret History of Freemasonry: Its Origins and Connection to the Knights Templar* (Rochester, Vt.: Inner Traditions, 2005).

Possel, Markus, and Ron Amundson. "Senior Researcher Comments on the Hundredth Monkey Phenomenon in Japan." *Skeptical Inquirer,* May/June 1996.

Pye, Michael, and Kirsten Dalley, eds. *Exposed, Uncovered and Declassified: Lost Civilizations and Secrets of the Past* (Pompton Plains, N.J.: New Page Books, 2012).

Roberts, Scott Alan. *The Rise and Fall of the Nephilim: The Untold Story of Fallen Angels, Giants on the Earth, and Their Extraterrestrial Origin* (Pompton Plains, N.J.: New Page Books, 2012).

Rogers, Everett. *Diffusion of Innovations, Fifth Edition* (New York: Free Press, 2003).

Sams, Gregory. *Sun of God: Discovering the Self-Organizing Consciousness That Underlies Everything* (San Francisco, Calif.: Weiser Books, 2009).

Scranton, Laird. *The Cosmological Origins of Myth and Symbol: From the Dogon and Ancient Egypt to India, Tibet and China* (Rochester, Vt.: Inner Traditions, 2010).

———. *Sacred Symbols of the Dogon: The Key to Advanced Science in the Ancient Egyptian Hieroglyphs* (Rochester, Vt.: Inner Traditions, 2007).

———. *The Science of the Dogon: Decoding the African Mystery Tradition* (Rochester, Vt.: Inner Traditions, 2006).

Shanks, Herschel. "What Brings You Here?" *Biblical Archeology Review,* July/August 2013.

Sitchin, Zecharia. *There Were Gods Upon the Earth: Gods, Demigods, and Human Ancestry: The Evidence of Alien DNA* (Rochester, Vt.: Bear & Co., 2010).

Smith, Matt. "Ancient Tennessee Cave Paintings Show Deep Thinking By Natives." *CNN.com,* June 21, 2013.

Stewart, Pete. *The Spiritual Science of the Stars: A Guide To the Architecture of the Spirit* (Rochester, Vt.: Inner Traditions, 2007).

Thagard, Paul. "Hot Thought: Why Memes Are a Bad Idea." *Psychology Today,* January 2013.

Von Daniken, Erich. *Odyssey of the Gods: The History of Extraterrestrial Contact in Ancient Greece* (Franklin Lakes, N.J.: New Page Books, 2010).

Von Franz, Marie-Louise. *The Interpretation of Fairy Tales* (Berkeley, Calif.: Shambhala Books, 1996).

Watts, Duncan J. *Everything Is Obvious: Why Common Sense Fails Us* (New York: Crown Books, 2012).

Woollaston, Victoria. "America's Oldest Cave Paintings Found, Dating Back Six Thousand Years." *UK Mail* online, June 18, 2013.

Index

※

About the Authors

Marie D. Jones

Marie D. Jones is the best-selling author of *Destiny vs. Choice: The Scientific and Spiritual Evidence Behind Fate and Free Will; 2013: End of Days or a New Beginning—Envisioning the World After the Events of 2012; PSIence: How New Discoveries in Quantum Physics and New Science May Explain the Existence of Paranormal Phenomena;* and *Looking for God in All the Wrong Places.* Marie coauthored with her father, geophysicist Dr. John Savino, *Supervolcano: The Catastrophic Event That Changed the Course of Human History.* She is also the coauthor of *11:11—The Time Prompt Phenomenon: The Meaning Behind Mysterious Signs, Sequences and Synchronicities; The Resonance Key: Exploring the Links Between Vibration, Consciousness, and the Zero Point Grid; The Déjà vu Enigma: A Journey Through the Anomalies of Mind, Memory. and Time;* and *The Trinity Secret: The Power of Three and the Code of Creation* with Larry Flaxman, her partner in ParaExplorers.com, an organization devoted to exploring unknown mysteries. Their latest book is *This Book Is From the Future: A Journey Through Portals, Relativity, Wormholes and Other Adventures in Time Travel.* Marie and Larry have also launched the ParaExplorer Series of e-books and articles introducing readers to a variety of subjects.

She has an extensive background in metaphysics, cutting-edge science, and the paranormal, and has worked as a field investigator for MUFON (Mutual UFO Network) in Los Angeles and San Diego in the 1980s and 1990s. She currently serves as a consultant and director of special projects for ARPAST, the Arkansas Paranormal and Anomalous Studies Team, where she works with ARPAST President Larry Flaxman to develop theories that can be tested in the field. Their current project, called The Grid, launched in 2013.

Marie has been on television, most recently on the History Channel's *Nostradamus Effect* series and *Ancient Aliens* series, and served as a special UFO/abduction consultant for the 2009 Universal Pictures science fiction movie *The Fourth Kind.* She has been interviewed on hundreds of radio talk shows all over the world, including *Coast to Coast* AM, NPR, KPBS Radio, *Dreamland, the X-Zone, Kevin Smith Show, Paranormal Podcast, Cut to the Chase, Feet 2 The Fire, World of the Unexplained,* and the *Shirley MacLaine Show,* and has been featured in dozens of newspapers, magazines, and online publications all over the world. She is a staff writer and official blogger for *Intrepid Magazine,* and a regular contributor to *New Dawn Magazine,* and her essays and articles have appeared in *TAPS ParaMagazine, Phenomena, Whole Life Times, Light Connection, Vision, Conspiracy Journal, Beyond Reality,* and several popular anthologies, such as *If Women Ruled the World, Let Go! And Let Miracles Happen,* three *Hot Chocolate for the Soul* books, and five *Chicken Soup for the Soul* books. She has also contributed and co-authored more than 50 inspirational books for New Seasons/PIL.

She has lectured widely at major metaphysical, paranormal, new science and self-empowerment events, including Through the Veil, Queen Mary Weekends, TAPS Academy Training, CPAK, and Paradigm Symposium, Conscious Expo, and Darkness Radio Events, and is a popular public speaker on the subjects of cutting-edge science, the paranormal, metaphysics, Noetics, and human potential. She speaks often at local metaphysical centers, churches, local libraries, bookstore signings, film festivals, and regional meet-ups on writing, the paranormal, human consciousness, science, and metaphysical subjects.

She is also the screenwriter and co-producer of *19 Hz,* a paranormal thriller in development with Bruce Lucas Films, as well as a science fiction feature film titled *Aurora,* and she serves as a co-host on the popular Dreamland Radio Show.

Larry Flaxman

Larry Flaxman is the best-selling author of *11:11—The Time Prompt Phenomenon: The Meaning Behind Mysterious Signs, Sequences and Synchronicities; The Resonance Key: Exploring the Links Between Vibration, Consciousness, and the Zero Point Grid; The Déjà vu Enigma: A Journey Through the Anomalies of Mind, Memory, and Time;* and *The Trinity Secret: The Power of Three and the Code of Creation* with Marie D. Jones, his partner in ParaExplorers.com. Their latest book is *This Book Is From the Future: A Journey Through Portals, Relativity, Wormholes and Other Adventures in Time Travel.*

Larry has been actively involved in paranormal research and hands-on field investigation for more than 13 years, and melds his technical, scientific, and investigative backgrounds together for no-nonsense, scientifically objective explanations regarding a variety of anomalous phenomena. He is the president and senior researcher of ARPAST, the Arkansas Paranormal and Anomalous Studies Team, which he founded in February 2007. Under his leadership, ARPAST has become one of the nation's largest and most active paranormal research organizations, with more than 150 members worldwide. Widely respected for his expertise on the proper use of equipment and techniques for conducting a solid investigation, Larry also serves as technical advisor to several paranormal research groups throughout the country.

Larry has appeared on Discovery Channel's *Ghost Lab* and History Channel's *Ancient Aliens* series, and has been interviewed for dozens of print and online publications, including *The Anomalist, Times Herald News, Jacksonville Patriot, ParaWeb, Current Affairs Herald, Unexplained Magazine,* the *Petit Jean County Headlight,* the *Villager Online,* and the *Pine Bluff Commercial.* He has appeared on hundreds of radio programs all over the world, including *Coast to Coast with George Noory, TAPS Family Radio, Encounters Radio, Higher Dimensions, X-Zone, Ghostly Talk, Eerie Radio, Crossroads Paranormal, Binall of America, World of the Unexplained,* and *Haunted Voices.*

Larry is a staff writer and official blogger for *Intrepid Magazine,* and his work has appeared regularly in *TAPS ParaMagazine, New Dawn Magazine,* and *Phenomena.* He is also a screenwriter, with a paranormal thriller, *19 Hz,* in development with Bruce Lucas Films, and a popular public speaker, lecturing widely at paranormal and metaphysical conferences and events all over the country, including major appearances at Through the Veil; History, Haunts and Legends; Paradigm Symposium; ESP Weekend at the Crescent Hotel; "The Texas GhostShow; and DragonCon. He also speaks widely at local and regional meet-ups, bookstore signings, libraries, and events on the subjects of science, the paranormal, metaphysics, Noetics, and human potential. Larry is also active in the development of cutting-edge custom designed equipment for use in the field investigating environmental effects and anomalies that may contribute to our understanding of the paranormal.